THE PRINCETON REVIEW

PRESENTS

HEADLINES™

VOLUME 1

BY KAZ

TIMES
BOOKS

ISBN: 0-8129-2187-9

Manufactured in the United States of America
9 8 7 6 5 4 3 2
First Edition

Designed by M. Kristen Bearse and Naomi Osnos
Production by MM Design 2000, Inc.

How to Solve HeadLines™

1. Guess the words defined in the clues listed below the grid (designated A, B, C, etc.) and write each letter over the numbered dashes.

2. Next, transfer each letter in the clue to the square in the puzzle (the headline) with the same number as the dash.

3. Words in the headline are separated by black squares, and words can continue from one line in the headline to the next.

4. As you proceed you will be able to guess words in the headline and transfer letters back to the dashes in the clues.

5. The completed puzzle will read as a newspaper headline about an event in the year indicated.

Tips

• You're not going to know all the clues right off, but don't panic. Knowing just a few of the clues will give you a good start at solving the puzzle.

• *At the start write in only the answers to clues that you're reasonably sure of* . . . and transfer the letters to the headline.

• Now try to guess some of the words in the headline; write them in and transfer the letters back to the clues below. These additional letters will help you answer the clues.

• Work back and forth this way until the puzzle is completed.

• If the letters don't spell out a word when transferred to the grid, your answer is probably wrong.

• Notations to the clues:

(3 wds)   This notation after a clue means that the answer consists of three separate words. These words will run together without spacing. For example, THETHREEBEARS.

(full name)   This means that the answer will be both the first and last name of a person, without spacing. For example, ABRAHAMLINCOLN.

(hyph)   This means that the answer will be a hyphenated word, but without spacing. For example, NOHITTER.

- Always pay attention to the word endings of the clues. For example:

  If the clue is a verb ending in "ing," chances are that the answer will end in "ING."

  If the clue is a verb ending in the past tense "ed," the answer will generally end in "ED."

  If the clue is a plural, the answer will usually end with an "S."

  You can write these endings over the final dashes in the clue even before you've answered the clue and transfer them to the proper squares in the headline.

- Pay careful attention to the wording of the clue. For example, if the clue is "DeNiro *or* Redford," the answer will be "ROBERT" . . . but if the clue is "DeNiro *and* Redford," the answer will be "ROBERTS."

- There is *no* punctuation in the body of the puzzle except for a *hyphen* (which would be seen in a square). "JOHN'S" would appear "JOHNS," "IT'S" would appear "ITS," etc.

1

Y·E·A·R 1·5·1·9

1 F	2 H	3 A	4 F	5 E	6 B	7 G	8 A	9 D		10 E	11 G	
12 A	13 B	14 D	15 F		16 C	17 A	18 E	19 G	20 H	21 B		22 A
23 D		24 C	25 A	26 A	27 E	28 D		29 A	30 F	31 H		32 G
33 D	34 A	35 B	36 H	37 G	38 A	39 A	40 C	41 E	42 D	43 A		

A. Vatican ceiling painter ....
 $\overline{8}$ $\overline{26}$ $\overline{39}$ $\overline{25}$ $\overline{34}$ $\overline{43}$ $\overline{22}$ $\overline{3}$ $\overline{29}$
 $\overline{12}$ $\overline{38}$ $\overline{17}$

B. Piquancy; tang; relish; gusto ...
 $\overline{6}$ $\overline{13}$ $\overline{21}$ $\overline{35}$

C. Bart Simpson says "Don't have a
___, man" ....
 $\overline{16}$ $\overline{40}$ $\overline{24}$

D. Shrewd; keen in judgment;
sagacious ....
 $\overline{9}$ $\overline{23}$ $\overline{14}$ $\overline{33}$ $\overline{42}$ $\overline{28}$

E. Barrier Reef, Dane, Lakes, or
white shark ....
 $\overline{10}$ $\overline{18}$ $\overline{5}$ $\overline{41}$ $\overline{27}$

F. Seaver and Selleck ....
 $\overline{4}$ $\overline{30}$ $\overline{1}$ $\overline{15}$

G. One fourth of a gallon ....
 $\overline{32}$ $\overline{7}$ $\overline{37}$ $\overline{11}$ $\overline{19}$

H. Fall into a light sleep
unintentionally ....
 $\overline{31}$ $\overline{2}$ $\overline{36}$ $\overline{20}$

Y·E·A·R 3·2·3·B·C

1 E	2 B	3 G	4 G	5 G	6 E	7 A	8 I	9 A		10 C	11 A	12 D
	13 G	14 C	15 E	16 A	17 H		18 I	19 F		20 I	21 C	22 B
23 F		24 A	25 G		26 B	27 F	28 B	29 A	30 E	31 B	32 I	
33 D	34 A		35 C	36 E	37 H		38 B	39 I	40 E		41 G	42 C
	43 H	44 H	45 F	46 A	47 D	48 A	—	49 F	50 G	51 A	52 C	53 H

A. Clint Eastwood's homicide
   inspector (2 wds) ....
   ___ ___ ___ ___ ___ ___ ___ ___ ___
   7 24 46 34 29 11 16 51   9
                                      ___
                                       48

B. Spanish conquistador, he
   discovered the Pacific Ocean ....
   ___ ___ ___ ___ ___ ___
   26 38   2 28 31 22

C. Chain placed on the feet ....
   ___ ___ ___ ___ ___ ___
   42 21 35 10 52 14

D. Boston ___ Party ....
   ___ ___ ___
   47 12 33

E. Capital city of Montana ....
   ___ ___ ___ ___ ___ ___
   36 15 30 40   6   1

F. Solemn; serious; sedate ....
   ___ ___ ___ ___ ___
   19 49 27 45 23

G. Six-sided figure ....
   ___ ___ ___ ___ ___ ___ ___
   50   3   4   5 13 41 25

H. By the skin of your ___
   (narrowly, barely) ....
   ___ ___ ___ ___ ___
   43 53 37 17 44

I. Condescend; to think fit or in
   accordance with one's dignity ...
   ___ ___ ___ ___ ___
   20   8 18 39 32

3

Y·E·A·R 1·8·6·1

1 E	2 B	3 H	4 D	5 E	6 B	7 B	8 D	9 D	10 A	11 C		12 H	13 B	14 E
15 G	16 H	17 D	18 C	19 A	20 F	21 D	22 G		23 I	24 F	25 D	26 A	27 H	28 G
	29 I	30 E	31 G	32 A	33 A	34 H		35 F	36 I	37 C	38 A		39 I	40 E
41 C	42 F	43 A	44 B		45 D	46 G	47 H		48 I	49 F	50 B	51 C	52 D	53 H

A. 1930s design style; Chrysler Building is a prime example (2 wds) ....

32 19 38 10 43 33 26

B. Gershwin, Patton, or Custer .....

50 6 13 44 7 2

C. One who lives in wretched circumstances in order to hoard money ....

41 51 11 18 37

D. Unfavorable or unfortunate; improper ....

4 52 21 25 45 8 9 17

E. Main force or impact, as of an attack ....

1 5 40 14 30

F. "... and they lived happily ever ___" ....

20 35 42 49 24

G. Banquet; abundant meal; something highly agreeable ......

15 22 46 28 31

H. Green Bay's NFL team ....

27 3 12 34 16 47 53

I. Small ships ....

48 36 29 23 39

4

Y·E·A·R 1·9·6·2

1 A	2 G	3 C	4 B	5 A	6 G	7 D	8 C	9 F	10 H		11 H	12 G
13 D	14 A	15 H	16 E		17 D	18 C		19 B	20 D	21 E	22 G	23 F
24 D		25 A	26 H	27 B	28 D	29 A		30 A	31 A	32 B	33 F	34 E
35 F	36 C	37 E		38 B	39 F		40 A	41 E	42 H	43 C	44 F	45 A

A. "Bette Davis Eyes" was her 1981 Grammy-winning record (full name) ....
<u>1</u> <u>31</u> <u>30</u> <u>25</u> <u>45</u> <u>40</u> <u>29</u> <u>14</u> <u>5</u>

B. Reynolds and Lancaster ....
<u>27</u> <u>4</u> <u>19</u> <u>38</u> <u>32</u>

C. "... my kingdom for a ____!" ("Richard III" V, iv) ....
<u>8</u> <u>18</u> <u>3</u> <u>43</u> <u>36</u>

D. Formally withdraw or disavow a statement or opinion; retract; rescind ....
<u>13</u> <u>20</u> <u>7</u> <u>28</u> <u>24</u> <u>17</u>

E. Spades, hearts, diamonds, and clubs ....
<u>16</u> <u>41</u> <u>34</u> <u>21</u> <u>37</u>

F. Houston's NFL team ....
<u>39</u> <u>44</u> <u>35</u> <u>9</u> <u>23</u> <u>33</u>

G. ____ Capet (king of France 987-96, founder of Capetian dynasty) ....
<u>6</u> <u>22</u> <u>12</u> <u>2</u>

H. Sophisticated; blandly urbane; smoothly polite ....
<u>42</u> <u>26</u> <u>11</u> <u>10</u> <u>15</u>

5

Y·E·A·R 1·9·9·1

1 A	2 B	3 A	4 E	5 B	6 C		7 F	8 B	9 A	10 G	11 G	12 E
13 D	■	14 H	15 A	16 F	17 H	18 G	19 I	20 B		21 G	22 D	23 A
24 B	25 I		26 C	27 G	28 A	29 B		30 D	31 A	32 A	33 B	
34 C	35 A	36 E	37 I	38 B	39 D		40 A	41 B	42 I	43 C	44 A	45 F
	46 A	47 A		48 E	49 H	50 D	51 A	52 B	53 F	54 A	55 C	

A. International association of
countries formed after WWI (3
wds) .... $\overline{3}$ $\overline{44}$ $\overline{28}$ $\overline{9}$ $\overline{23}$ $\overline{35}$ $\overline{15}$ $\overline{47}$ $\overline{54}$

$\overline{1}$ $\overline{32}$ $\overline{31}$ $\overline{46}$ $\overline{40}$ $\overline{51}$

B. Release or let go of; yield;
cede; forego .... $\overline{38}$ $\overline{5}$ $\overline{2}$ $\overline{52}$ $\overline{24}$ $\overline{29}$ $\overline{41}$ $\overline{8}$ $\overline{20}$

$\overline{33}$

C. "___ of a feather flock
together" .... $\overline{43}$ $\overline{26}$ $\overline{34}$ $\overline{6}$ $\overline{55}$

D. It hung by a hair over the head
of Damocles .... $\overline{50}$ $\overline{30}$ $\overline{22}$ $\overline{13}$ $\overline{39}$

E. Mickey and Minnie .... $\overline{48}$ $\overline{4}$ $\overline{36}$ $\overline{12}$

F. Shape of a thing or person;
dressmaker's dummy .... $\overline{7}$ $\overline{53}$ $\overline{45}$ $\overline{16}$

G. Capital of the state of Western
Australia .... $\overline{21}$ $\overline{18}$ $\overline{27}$ $\overline{11}$ $\overline{10}$

H. Cloth tied under the chin of a
child being fed .... $\overline{14}$ $\overline{49}$ $\overline{17}$

I. Where most college freshmen live $\overline{25}$ $\overline{37}$ $\overline{19}$ $\overline{42}$

6

Y·E·A·R 1·9·5·9

1 K	2 F	3 D	4 E	5 I	6 H	7 A		8 C	9 B	10 G	11 A	12 F			13 H
14 D	15 D	16 J			17 C	18 H	19 B	20 F	21 E			22 C	23 H	24 G	25 A	26 D
27 B			28 H	29 C	30 B	31 F	32 G		33 C	34 B	35 A	36 F	37 D	38 J		
39 K	40 A	41 J		42 F	43 J	44 J	45 B	46 D	47 A	48 I	49 D	50 F	51 A	52 K	
	53 F	54 E	55 I		56 F	57 D	58 F	59 K	60 A	61 B	62 G	63 I	64 E	65 F	

A. Bearing upon the matter at hand; pertinent; germane ....
 $\overline{60}$ $\overline{11}$ $\overline{47}$ $\overline{51}$ $\overline{35}$ $\overline{7}$ $\overline{40}$ $\overline{25}$

B. Where baseball's Athletics play .
 $\overline{27}$ $\overline{34}$ $\overline{30}$ $\overline{9}$ $\overline{45}$ $\overline{61}$ $\overline{19}$

C. Separate the wheat from the ___ (eliminate the unimportant) .....
 $\overline{22}$ $\overline{33}$ $\overline{29}$ $\overline{8}$ $\overline{17}$

D. Unreasonably obstinate; unyielding, headstrong, resolute
 $\overline{49}$ $\overline{3}$ $\overline{14}$ $\overline{46}$ $\overline{15}$ $\overline{57}$ $\overline{26}$ $\overline{37}$

E. Longest river in the world ......
 $\overline{64}$ $\overline{4}$ $\overline{21}$ $\overline{54}$

F. "Hark! hark! the lark at ____ sings" (2 wds; "Cymbeline" II, iii) ....
 $\overline{50}$ $\overline{20}$ $\overline{36}$ $\overline{58}$ $\overline{42}$ $\overline{53}$ $\overline{12}$ $\overline{56}$ $\overline{2}$
 $\overline{65}$ $\overline{31}$

G. Dirty or untidy condition ....
 $\overline{62}$ $\overline{10}$ $\overline{24}$ $\overline{32}$

H. Part of a house directly under a roof; garret ....
 $\overline{23}$ $\overline{28}$ $\overline{6}$ $\overline{18}$ $\overline{13}$

I. Intelligent; sagacious ....
 $\overline{55}$ $\overline{48}$ $\overline{5}$ $\overline{63}$

J. He made the first visit to Israel by an Arab leader ....
 $\overline{43}$ $\overline{38}$ $\overline{41}$ $\overline{16}$ $\overline{44}$

K. Foundation ....
 $\overline{1}$ $\overline{39}$ $\overline{52}$ $\overline{59}$

7

Y·E·A·R 1·7·7·5

1 B	2 F	3 I	4 B		5 G	6 A	7 H	8 B	9 E	10 H		11 D	12 A
13 I	14 F	15 J		16 H	17 I	18 D	19 A		20 A	21 I	22 C	23 E	24 A
25 B		26 J	27 E		28 A	29 C	30 C	31 B	32 E	33 F	34 G	35 J	36 F
	37 A	38 G		39 F	40 C	41 H	42 B		43 E	44 D		45 A	46 F
47 H	48 C	49 F	50 H	51 H		52 B	53 D	54 F	55 A	56 E	57 B	58 H	

A. Bruce Wayne's "wheels" ....
__45__ __55__ __37__ __19__ __24__ __20__ __12__ __28__ __6__

B. Highest point ....
__1__ __31__ __42__ __25__ __52__ __57__ __4__ __8__

C. Lone Star State ....
__48__ __29__ __30__ __40__ __22__

D. Inventor Henry or motion picture director John ....
__44__ __18__ __11__ __53__

E. Sewer worker character in "The Honeymooners" ....
__32__ __43__ __9__ __23__ __27__ __56__

F. Vacillating; fluctuating ....
__39__ __2__ __54__ __14__ __46__ __49__ __36__ __33__

G. Decay ....
__5__ __38__ __34__

H. Excited, restless or uncontrolled ....
__16__ __58__ __7__ __10__ __41__ __47__ __50__ __51__

I. Sullen; severe; stern ....
__13__ __21__ __3__ __17__

J. Chronic drunkard ....
__15__ __35__ __26__

Y·E·A·R 1·9·4·3

1 B	2 F	3 F	4 A	5 G	6 E	7 B	8 H	9 F		10 A	11 C	12 G
	13 B	14 G	15 E	16 B	17 A	18 E	19 A	20 E	21 A		22 A	23 A
24 E	25 A		26 C	27 B		28 G	29 E	30 A	31 H	32 E	33 B	34 G
35 H	36 H	37 G		38 D	39 E		40 A	41 G	42 E		43 B	44 F
45 G	46 D	47 E	48 B		49 A	50 E	51 C	52 B	53 D	54 A	55 C	56 D

A. Big Bird and Cookie Monster
live here (2 wds) ....
$\overline{30}\ \overline{54}\ \overline{40}\ \overline{10}\ \overline{22}\ \overline{17}\ \overline{49}\ \overline{25}\ \overline{4}$
$\overline{19}\ \overline{23}\ \overline{21}$

B. They elect the pope; they play
football in Phoenix ....
$\overline{1}\ \overline{43}\ \overline{13}\ \overline{48}\ \overline{7}\ \overline{27}\ \overline{52}\ \overline{33}\ \overline{16}$

C. "With this ___ I thee wed" ......
$\overline{51}\ \overline{26}\ \overline{11}\ \overline{55}$

D. ___-bitty ....
$\overline{46}\ \overline{53}\ \overline{38}\ \overline{56}$

E. TV series with "Captain" Gavin
McLeod, 1977-86 (3 wds) ....
$\overline{42}\ \overline{6}\ \overline{47}\ \overline{20}\ \overline{15}\ \overline{18}\ \overline{24}\ \overline{32}\ \overline{39}$
$\overline{29}\ \overline{50}$

F. Cordell ____ (US Secretary of
State 1933-44; Nobel peace
prize 1945) ....
$\overline{2}\ \overline{3}\ \overline{9}\ \overline{44}$

G. Any honor or award; ceremony
used in conferring knighthood ...
$\overline{34}\ \overline{28}\ \overline{5}\ \overline{14}\ \overline{45}\ \overline{37}\ \overline{12}\ \overline{41}$

H. Group of people of common
descent, as in the Scottish
Highlands ....
$\overline{36}\ \overline{8}\ \overline{31}\ \overline{35}$

9

Y·E·A·R 1·8·8·0

		1 C	2 C	3 A	4 G	5 G	6 E	7 B	8 A	9 B		10 H	11 G
	12 B	13 F	14 G	15 G	16 H	17 A	18 F		19 C	20 A		21 E	22 A
23 F	24 A	25 B	26 G	27 C	28 C	29 F		30 G	31 G	32 D	33 E		34 F
35 B	36 G	37 D		38 C	39 A	40 A	41 H		42 A	43 A	44 C		45 A
46 A	47 G	48 D	49 B	50 C	51 A		52 G	53 E	54 B	55 C	56 A		

A. "... the face that launch'd
____" (3 wds; Marlowe, "Doctor
Faustus") .... __ __ __ __ __ __ __ __ __
  8 3 45 22 46 56 40 17 51

  __ __ __ __ __
  42 39 43 24 20

B. He wrote "Alice in Wonderland" .. __ __ __ __ __ __ __
  12 54 49 7 35 25 9

C. Free from a difficulty or
entanglement .... __ __ __ __ __ __ __ __ __
  28 44 38 55 19 1 2 27 50

D. "___ on a Grecian Urn" (poem by
Keats) .... __ __ __
  32 48 37

E. "The boy stood on the burning
___/Whence all but he had fled
(Hemans, "Casabianca") .... __ __ __ __
  6 53 21 33

F. Electronic device used to
transmit computer data by
telephone .... __ __ __ __ __
  34 13 29 18 23

G. The woman described in Clue A
(3 wds) .... __ __ __ __ __ __ __ __ __
  4 26 14 5 47 31 11 30 36

  __ __
  15 52

H. Beverage made with beaten eggs,
usually with alcoholic liquor ... __ __ __
  41 10 16

10

1 H	2 A	3 D	4 E	5 C	6 B	7 D	8 H		9 I	10 A	11 K	12 C
	13 H	14 G	15 B		16 F	17 E	18 G	19 C	20 B		21 J	22 J
23 J	24 C	25 D	26 K		27 J	28 F	29 D		30 A	31 B	32 J	33 F
	34 H	35 B		36 K	37 A	38 H	39 L	40 G	41 B	42 K	43 H	44 A
	45 F	46 I	47 B	48 D	49 E		50 H	51 L	52 B	53 C	54 H	55 L
56 J		57 D	58 A	59 H	60 J	61 B		62 A	63 H	64 E	65 B	66 A
67 H	68 C		69 B	70 A	71 J	72 B		73 H	74 I	75 H	76 D	77 J

A. Husband of Nicole Kidman (full name) .... $\overline{62}$ $\overline{10}$ $\overline{44}$ $\overline{30}$ $\overline{66}$ $\overline{70}$ $\overline{58}$ $\overline{2}$ $\overline{37}$

B. Theory that government should not interfere in economic affairs (2 wds) .... $\overline{6}$ $\overline{65}$ $\overline{31}$ $\overline{69}$ $\overline{20}$ $\overline{15}$ $\overline{72}$ $\overline{35}$ $\overline{41}$

$\overline{61}$ $\overline{52}$ $\overline{47}$

C. Not sharp; dull in perception; unfeeling .... $\overline{53}$ $\overline{19}$ $\overline{12}$ $\overline{24}$ $\overline{68}$ $\overline{5}$

D. Commended; lauded; expressed approval .... $\overline{25}$ $\overline{3}$ $\overline{76}$ $\overline{7}$ $\overline{57}$ $\overline{48}$ $\overline{29}$

E. ___ speed (Fast as the Enterprise can go) .... $\overline{64}$ $\overline{4}$ $\overline{17}$ $\overline{49}$

F. Kill by violence .... $\overline{45}$ $\overline{28}$ $\overline{16}$ $\overline{33}$

G. Powdery residue of matter that remains after burning .... $\overline{18}$ $\overline{40}$ $\overline{14}$

H. "Now is the winter of _____" (2 wds; "Richard III I, i) .... $\overline{34}$ $\overline{54}$ $\overline{38}$ $\overline{67}$ $\overline{1}$ $\overline{8}$ $\overline{73}$ $\overline{63}$ $\overline{59}$

$\overline{50}$ $\overline{43}$ $\overline{75}$ $\overline{13}$

I. Crude; not refined by art or taste; uncooked .... $\overline{9}$ $\overline{74}$ $\overline{46}$

J. One of the most popular dessert flavors .... $\overline{23}$ $\overline{56}$ $\overline{27}$ $\overline{22}$ $\overline{21}$ $\overline{77}$ $\overline{60}$ $\overline{32}$ $\overline{71}$

K. Bastille Day is the 14th of this month .... $\overline{36}$ $\overline{11}$ $\overline{42}$ $\overline{26}$

L. Embrace; keep close to; cling fondly .... $\overline{51}$ $\overline{39}$ $\overline{55}$

11

Y·E·A·R 1·7·7·5

		1 E	2 C	3 A	4 D	5 F		6 B	7 F	8 E	9 A	10 B	11 F
	12 C	13 D	14 A	15 A	16 G		17 A	18 F	19 B	20 A	21 A	22 C	23 G
24 F		25 D	26 A	27 A	28 H		29 C	30 A	31 B	32 D	33 H		34 D
35 A	36 F	37 A	38 A	39 B	40 F		41 A	42 F	43 A	44 B		45 H	46 A
	47 H	48 D	49 F	50 A	51 D	52 E	53 C	54 A	55 D	56 G	57 E		

A. Sinatra played Maggio in 1953 film of James Jones novel of army life (4 wds) ....
41 35 50 17 3 30 54 9 46
26 14 21 15 43 20 38 37
27

B. State capital of Texas ....
6 19 39 44 31 10

C. "All the world's a ____" ("As You Like It" II, vii) ....
29 2 22 12 53

D. School of painters (Corot, Millet, Rousseau, etc.) ....
34 4 13 25 48 32 55 51

E. Go before; show the way ....
8 1 57 52

F. He played the Joker in "Batman" .
24 36 49 40 18 7 11 42 5

G. Eli Whitney's machine for separating cotton fibers from the seeds ....
56 23 16

H. Right to the privileges of membership in a stock exchange ..
28 33 45 47

12

Y·E·A·R 1·9·5·3

1 E	2 H	3 A	4 I	5 D	6 J	7 G		8 G	9 E	10 A	11 D	12 I	13 B
14 G		15 A	16 I	17 E	18 H	19 G	20 B	21 E	22 I		23 A	24 F	25 C
26 B	27 A	28 F	29 G	30 D	31 C	32 B		33 A	34 A	35 C		36 A	37 J
38 B	39 C	40 G	41 A	42 J	43 D	44 B		45 I	46 A	47 D	48 A	49 C	50 A
	51 H	52 F	53 B	54 A	55 D		56 F	57 E	58 A	59 I	60 F	61 B	

A. Long John Silver appears in this Stevenson novel (2 wds) ....
___ ___ ___ ___ ___ ___ ___ ___ ___
3 50 54 15 58 10 23 46 36
___ ___ ___ ___ ___
41 27 33 34 48

B. Ancient Greek god of the sea ....
___ ___ ___ ___ ___ ___ ___ ___
38 26 44 13 20 53 61 32

C. Straits between England and France ....
___ ___ ___ ___ ___
35 31 25 49 39

D. Little boys are made of "snips and ___ and puppy dogs' tails" ..
___ ___ ___ ___ ___ ___
5 43 47 30 55 11

E. Well done! Great! (a shout in approbation) ....
___ ___ ___ ___ ___
1 9 57 21 17

F. Polish-born French physicist (1867-1934), she isolated radium
___ ___ ___ ___ ___
56 28 60 52 24

G. Lacking movement, development or vitality; showing little or no change ....
___ ___ ___ ___ ___ ___
14 19 7 29 40 8

H. So ___ so good (no difficulty up to the present) ....
___ ___ ___
51 2 18

I. Carefree; cheerful; sprightly; light-hearted ....
___ ___ ___ ___ ___ ___
16 45 4 59 12 22

J. Hanks or Cruise ....
___ ___ ___
6 42 37

13

Y·E·A·R B·I·B·L·I·C·A·L

	1 F	2 D	3 C	4 A	5 G		6 F	7 D	8 C	9 E	10 A	11 D
12 C		13 G	14 F	15 C	16 D	17 H	18 D	19 A		20 G	21 I	22 B	23 D
24 H		25 E	26 F	27 D		28 E	29 H	30 I	31 A	32 E		33 H	34 B
35 G	36 I		37 D	38 A	39 H		40 H	41 I	42 A	43 B	44 E	45 H	46 E
47 A	48 D		49 F	50 E		51 B	52 D	53 G	54 C	55 A	56 E	

A. Longtime head coach of the Miami Dolphins (full name) ······ `___ ___ ___ ___ ___ ___ ___ ___`
31 4 47 19 38 42 10 55

B. California's wine-making valley . `___ ___ ___ ___`
43 22 34 51

C. Close friend; chum; buddy ······· `___ ___ ___ ___ ___`
15 54 3 8 12

D. Hemingway gangster story; 1946 Burt Lancaster film (2 wds) ····· `___ ___ ___ ___ ___ ___ ___ ___ ___`
37 23 16 27 7 11 2 18 52

`___`
48

E. One who believes that all events are subject to inevitable predetermination ····· `___ ___ ___ ___ ___ ___ ___ ___`
50 9 44 25 28 46 32 56

F. Propose or volunteer to do something ······················· `___ ___ ___ ___ ___`
49 1 6 14 26

G. Beautify; deck; enhance ········· `___ ___ ___ ___ ___`
53 5 35 13 20

H. Wolfgang ____ Mozart ··········· `___ ___ ___ ___ ___ ___ ___`
45 40 29 17 39 33 24

I. Midday ························· `___ ___ ___ ___`
30 21 41 36

14

Y·E·A·R 1·8·4·0

1 D	2 G	3 H	4 I	5 L	6 F		7 A	8 E		9 C	10 K	11 B
12 I	■	13 H	14 A	15 C	16 F	17 H	18 D		19 I	20 E	21 K	22 C
23 B	24 G	25 A		26 F	27 C	28 E	29 G	30 J		31 K	32 I	33 A
34 I	35 L	36 D	37 I	38 H		39 G	40 D	41 E	42 J	43 I	44 G	45 C
	46 I	47 A	48 K	49 L	50 K	51 F		52 D	53 C	54 A	55 B	56 F
57 I	58 E		59 J	60 G		61 C	62 K	63 K	64 J	65 B	66 A	67 C

A. American who won his first Wimbledon singles title in 1974 .
___ ___ ___ ___ ___ ___ ___
33 14 66 54   7 47 25

B. Germany, Italy, and Japan in WWII ....
___ ___ ___ ___
65 11 23 55

C. "Gather ye ___ while ye may,/Old Time is still a-flying" (Herrick) ....
___ ___ ___ ___ ___ ___ ___ ___
22 53 45 61 15 27 67   9

D. She became Princess ____ when she married Rainier III in 1956 .
___ ___ ___ ___ ___
18 36   1 52 40

E. Aspect; phase; small, polished plane surface of a cut gem ......
___ ___ ___ ___ ___
 8 20 41 28 58

F. Repeat words from a book, speech, etc. ....
___ ___ ___ ___ ___
26 16 56   6 51

G. Frail; infirm; weak ....
___ ___ ___ ___ ___ ___
60 44 24 39   2 29

H. Constellation or sign Cancer ....
___ ___ ___ ___
13 17 38   3

I. TV's evening hours (2 wds) ......
___ ___ ___ ___ ___ ___ ___ ___ ___
46 57 32 19   4 34 37 43 12

J. Web-footed, fish-eating diving bird ....
___ ___ ___ ___
64 42 59 30

K. Yearning; hungering for ....
___ ___ ___ ___ ___ ___ ___
50 21 10 31 48 62 63

L. Used in negative phrases, especially after "neither" ......
___ ___ ___
49 35   5

15

Y·E·A·R 1·4·1·5

	1 E	2 G	3 B	4 H	5 D	6 D	7 I		8 G	9 B	10 H	11 A
12 F	13 D		14 I	15 E	16 D	17 A	18 F		19 J	20 B	21 I	22 C
23 A		24 E		25 B	26 J	27 G	28 J		29 E	30 F	31 C	
32 B	33 A	34 D	35 G	36 F	37 C		38 D	39 I	40 A	41 G		42 B
43 D		44 C	45 H	46 H	47 D	48 J	49 I	50 J	51 D	52 C		

A. "Yet I shall temper so/Justice with ___" (Milton, "Paradise Lost") ....
___ ___ ___ ___ ___
40 17 33 11 23

B. Wander in search of supplies; seek; rummage ....
___ ___ ___ ___ ___ ___
32 9 25 42 3 20

C. "Absence makes the ____ grow fonder" ....
___ ___ ___ ___ ___
37 31 44 22 52

D. She spells her name "Barbra" ....
___ ___ ___ ___ ___ ___ ___ ___ ___
13 43 51 34 5 6 38 47 16

E. Give free play or expression to an emotion, passion, etc. ....
___ ___ ___ ___
24 1 15 29

F. She won the 1987 Best Actress Oscar for "Moonstruck" ....
___ ___ ___ ___
36 30 12 18

G. Amusing; comical ....
___ ___ ___ ___ ___
8 27 2 35 41

H. "There was a little ___/Who had a little curl" (Longfellow) .....
___ ___ ___ ___
45 46 10 4

I. One of the Great Lakes ....
___ ___ ___ ___ ___
7 14 39 49 21

J. ___ and go (a precarious or delicate state of affairs) ......
___ ___ ___ ___ ___
28 26 50 48 19

Y·E·A·R 1·9·4·3

	1 A	2 G	3 D	4 B	5 I	6 H	7 A	8 B	9 D		10 E	11 C	12 B	13 G
14 F	15 A	16 E	17 H	18 C		19 D	20 A	21 B		22 B	23 F	24 A	25 G	26 E
27 E		28 G	29 F	30 I	31 D		32 G	33 A		34 G	35 A	36 B	37 I	38 C
	39 A	40 D	41 H		42 G	43 E	44 I	45 D	46 H		47 B	48 H	49 G	
50 C	51 A	52 I	53 I	54 I	55 G		56 A	57 D	58 B	59 E	60 A	61 F		

A. Norway, Sweden, Denmark, Finland (and sometimes Iceland), as a group .... `39` `1` `60` `33` `56` `24` `20` `51` `15`

`7` `35`

B. Playwright Odets (his works include "Golden Boy" and "Awake and Sing") .... `22` `8` `36` `47` `58` `12` `4` `21`

C. Japanese general who ordered the attack on Pearl Harbor ...... `18` `11` `50` `38`

D. Strive to equal or excel, usually through imitation .... `40` `45` `3` `9` `19` `31` `57`

E. Go back on one's word .... `10` `16` `26` `59` `27` `43`

F. Objective case of "thou" .... `61` `23` `29` `14`

G. Not even a mouse was stirring on this evening before _____ .... `34` `2` `49` `32` `55` `42` `28` `25` `13`

H. Indolence; laziness; animal that hangs upside down on tree branches .... `46` `17` `48` `41` `6`

I. One of Santa's reindeer .... `52` `44` `53` `54` `5` `30` `37`

17

Y·E·A·R 1·9·8·8

	1 F	2 B	3 H	4 H	5 H	6 A	7 I		8 H	9 F	10 F	11 B
12 I	13 C		14 E	15 G		16 F	17 A	18 B	19 C	20 I		21 A
22 G	23 B	24 E	25 G		26 D	27 H	28 B	29 H	30 A		31 F	32 F
33 B	34 C	35 F		36 G	37 B	38 H	39 I	40 A	41 C	42 B	43 E	
44 D	45 C		46 B	47 A	48 D	49 E	50 F	51 A	52 A	53 C		

A. 1940 Walt Disney film, cartoon animation set to classical music

$\overline{21}\ \overline{17}\ \overline{30}\ \overline{51}\ \overline{47}\ \overline{40}\ \overline{6}\ \overline{52}$

B. Evening broadcasting hours (2 wds) ....

$\overline{46}\ \overline{23}\ \overline{37}\ \overline{18}\ \overline{42}\ \overline{11}\ \overline{33}\ \overline{28}\ \overline{2}$

C. Instigate; stir up ....

$\overline{45}\ \overline{13}\ \overline{34}\ \overline{19}\ \overline{53}\ \overline{41}$

D. Bowl-shaped pan used in cooking Chinese food ....

$\overline{26}\ \overline{44}\ \overline{48}$

E. Colored portion of the eye ......

$\overline{14}\ \overline{43}\ \overline{49}\ \overline{24}$

F. Actresses Audrey and Katharine ..

$\overline{9}\ \overline{35}\ \overline{31}\ \overline{1}\ \overline{10}\ \overline{32}\ \overline{16}\ \overline{50}$

G. Thin fog; drizzle; cloud ....

$\overline{36}\ \overline{22}\ \overline{15}\ \overline{25}$

H. Source of great and sudden wealth; a spectacular windfall ..

$\overline{8}\ \overline{27}\ \overline{3}\ \overline{29}\ \overline{38}\ \overline{5}\ \overline{4}$

I. Dish the ____ (gossip) ....

$\overline{20}\ \overline{39}\ \overline{7}\ \overline{12}$

18

Y·E·A·R 1·9·9·1

	1 G	2 A	3 D	4 A	5 B	6 F			7 E	8 G	9 E	10 F			11 C	12 G
13 A	14 D			15 E	16 C	17 G	18 B	19 A	20 C	21 H	22 A			23 G	24 H	
25 E	26 D	27 C	28 E	29 A	30 B			31 B	32 F	33 G			34 A	35 C	36 E	
37 B	38 D	39 E	40 B			41 H	42 A	43 F			44 A	45 G	46 D	47 C	48 E	

A. He became Chief Justice of the
US Supreme Court in 1986 .... ___ ___ ___ ___ ___ ___ ___ ___ ___
                                    2   29   44   42   4   13   19   22   34

B. Giving or using in great
amounts; extravagant; unlimited . ___ ___ ___ ___ ___ ___
                                  30   37   40   5   18   31

C. Lindbergh, Byrd, Earhart, and
Post .... ___ ___ ___ ___ ___ ___
                                  47   20   16   35   27   11

D. Jefferson, Bette, or Miles ...... ___ ___ ___ ___ ___
                                  14   3   38   46   26

E. "I'll be seeing you in all the
old ____ places" .... ___ ___ ___ ___ ___ ___ ___ ___
                                  7   48   15   39   36   25   28   9

F. ____ effect (a drug's effect,
usually harmful, in addition to
its intended result) .... ___ ___ ___ ___
                                  6   32   43   10

G. Of or characteristic of the
largest continent .... ___ ___ ___ ___ ___ ___ ___
                                  23   17   1   45   33   8   12

H. It was dumped into Boston
harbor in 1773 .... ___ ___ ___
                                  24   21   41

19

Y·E·A·R 4·4·B·C

1 G	2 A	3 E	4 F	5 B	6 G		7 D	8 A	9 H	10 F		11 B	12 C	13 F
14 F	15 C	16 H	17 D	18 F	19 A	20 D	21 H		22 C	23 A	24 I	25 B	26 F	27 B
28 H		29 E	30 F	31 B	32 F	33 I		34 D	35 C		36 F	37 G	38 A	39 I
40 D		41 E	42 F	43 F	44 F		45 A	46 D	47 I		48 H	49 B	50 F	51 I

A. Soul diva Franklin .... __ __ __ __ __ __
  23 38 8 19 45 2

B. Under a cup .... __ __ __ __ __ __
  25 5 27 11 31 49

C. Fly the ___ (to escape; flee) ... __ __ __ __
  22 12 35 15

D. Skillful; clever; socially at
  ease .... __ __ __ __ __ __
  40 7 17 20 46 34

E. "For many are called, but ___
  are chosen" (Matthew 22:14) ..... __ __ __
  29 3 41

F. According to Longfellow, it was
  on his behalf that John Alden
  courted Priscilla (full name) ... __ __ __ __ __ __ __ __ __
  50 42 30 32 14 36 43 18 13

  __ __ __ __
  10 26 4 44

G. A far ___ (quite some distance) . __ __ __
  1 6 37

H. Madame Gorbachev .... __ __ __ __ __
  21 9 16 28 48

I. Timid or cowardly person; wimp .. __ __ __ __ __
  33 39 24 47 51

20

Y·E·A·R 1·9·4·3

1 D	2 E	3 A	4 D	5 H		6 B	7 B	8 A	9 I	10 J	11 D	12 F	13 A
14 I	15 J		16 B	17 C	18 B	19 D	20 H	21 C	22 F	23 A	24 B	25 I	26 F
27 C	28 E	29 J	30 G		31 D	32 B	33 C	34 G	35 D	36 F	37 B	38 A	39 I
	40 B	41 D	42 H	43 C	44 H	45 D		46 F	47 A	48 E	49 D	50 B	51 H
	52 G	53 F	54 B	55 C	56 D	57 F		58 B	59 D	60 H	61 G		62 H
63 C		64 D	65 A	66 B	67 J	68 F	69 J		70 C	71 I	72 E	73 A	

A. With a stated price for each dish on the menu (3 wds) ....
  65 47 3 38 73 8 23 13

B. Haughtily disdainful; arrogant; scornful ....
  6 16 66 50 32 18 24 58 37
  54 7 40

C. "Every woman should marry, ____" (3 wds; Disraeli) ....
  70 63 21 43 55 33 27 17

D. City where famous auto race is held every Memorial Day weekend .
  49 11 45 41 59 64 31 56 19
  4 1 35

E. Describe; impart; disclose ......
  2 72 28 48

F. Says Portia to Shylock: "The quality of mercy is not ____" ...
  57 36 53 46 22 26 68 12

G. Neat and orderly ....
  52 34 61 30

H. Disputing; withholding from .....
  51 44 20 5 62 60 42

I. Baseball fielder's misplay ......
  39 14 9 25 71

J. Persuades someone to buy something; convinces ....
  15 10 67 29 69

Y·E·A·R 3·3·4·B·C

1 J	2 G	3 D	4 A		5 B	6 G		7 D	8 G	9 A	10 C	11 F	12 K
13 A	14 I	15 I		16 E	17 D		18 I	19 A	20 C	21 J	22 G	23 D	24 E	25 A
26 C		27 J	28 I	29 K	30 K	31 H	32 I	33 E		34 A	35 B	36 C		37 H
38 G	39 A	40 B	41 H	42 G	43 F	44 E	45 A	46 C		47 G	48 J	49 J		50 A
51 B	52 I	53 J		54 K	55 G		56 K	57 E	58 F	59 A	60 I	61 B		

A. He created Mickey Mouse (full
name) .... $\overline{50}$ $\overline{19}$ $\overline{39}$ $\overline{34}$ $\overline{13}$ $\overline{25}$ $\overline{59}$ $\overline{45}$ $\overline{9}$

$\overline{4}$

B. "Hello," "welcome," or
"farewell" in Hawaii .... $\overline{51}$ $\overline{40}$ $\overline{5}$ $\overline{35}$ $\overline{61}$

C. Strictly accurate; precise ...... $\overline{36}$ $\overline{10}$ $\overline{26}$ $\overline{20}$ $\overline{46}$

D. The head on a glass of beer ..... $\overline{17}$ $\overline{23}$ $\overline{7}$ $\overline{3}$

E. Loop with a running knot, as in
a lasso .... $\overline{24}$ $\overline{44}$ $\overline{16}$ $\overline{33}$ $\overline{57}$

F. Average or normal .... $\overline{43}$ $\overline{11}$ $\overline{58}$

G. "In ___ fields the poppies
blow/Between the crosses, row
on row" (from a poem by John
McCrae) .... $\overline{6}$ $\overline{8}$ $\overline{47}$ $\overline{55}$ $\overline{22}$ $\overline{38}$ $\overline{2}$ $\overline{42}$

H. The woman in question .... $\overline{31}$ $\overline{37}$ $\overline{41}$

I. "The more the ___" .... $\overline{18}$ $\overline{32}$ $\overline{28}$ $\overline{52}$ $\overline{60}$ $\overline{14}$ $\overline{15}$

J. Move or climb upward .... $\overline{1}$ $\overline{53}$ $\overline{27}$ $\overline{21}$ $\overline{48}$ $\overline{49}$

K. Golf's number three wood .... $\overline{30}$ $\overline{56}$ $\overline{29}$ $\overline{54}$ $\overline{12}$

Y·E·A·R B·I·B·L·I·C·A·L

1 A	2 H	3 A	4 F	5 G	6 D	7 A	8 F	9 C	10 H	■	11 E	12 C
13 I	14 E	15 A	16 B	17 E	18 G	19 A	20 J	■	21 E	22 L	23 K	24 A
25 C	26 B	■	27 K	28 L	■	29 I	30 K	31 L	32 F	■	33 G	34 E
35 B	36 K	■	37 D	38 J	39 A	40 J	41 J	42 H	43 E	■	44 C	45 I
46 E	47 A	48 B	49 F	■	50 E	51 K	■	52 D	53 C	54 A	55 L	■
56 E	57 D	■	58 B	59 A	60 E	61 G	62 B	63 C	64 L	65 J	66 J	67 E

A. She won her first Wimbledon title in 1974 (full name) .... __47 __15 __1 __54 __39 __19 __3 __24 __59
__7

B. Philadelphia's NFL team .... __48 __58 __62 __35 __16 __26

C. Great warmth and earnestness of feeling; ardor; zeal .... __44 __63 __25 __53 __9 __12

D. Month, day, and year .... __37 __6 __57 __52

E. Julie Andrews, playing a British nanny, won the Oscar for this 1964 film (2 wds) ...... __60 __56 __46 __43 __21 __50 __14 __11 __34
__67 __17

F. "Beware the ___ of March" ("Julius Caesar" I, ii) .... __8 __32 __4 __49

G. "... and from the jail came the ___ of a downhearted frail" ("Birth of the Blues") .... __33 __61 __18 __5

H. Largest division of geologic time comprising two or more eras __2 __42 __10

I. Thick or sticky substance (informal) .... __29 __13 __45

J. Retained data in a memory unit .. __20 __40 __66 __41 __38 __65

K. "Who's Afraid of Virginia ___?" (Edward Albee's 1962 play) .... __23 __30 __27 __36 __51

L. "There is a tide in the affairs of men,/Which, taken at the ___, leads on to fortune" ("Julius Caesar") .... __28 __55 __22 __31 __64

23

Y·E·A·R 1·8·0·5

1 A	2 B	3 G	4 C	5 A	6 B	7 D	8 F	9 A		10 H	11 F	12 D	13 C
14 A	15 G	16 B	17 A	18 F	19 E	20 B		21 G	22 D	23 I	24 F	25 F	26 H
27 A	28 H		29 I	30 A	31 D	32 F	33 H	34 E	35 A	36 F		37 B	38 E	39 H
40 A	41 D	42 H	43 F	44 B	45 A	46 H		47 B	48 I	49 A	50 C	51 F	52 A
53 G	54 E		55 D	56 H	57 I	58 A	59 H	60 D	61 B	62 A	63 H	64 C

A. Robert Louis Stevenson's story about Jim Hawkins and the pirates (2 wds) ....
 58 40 27 45 9 30 49 17 62
 52 5 35 1 14

B. Point beyond which bombers cannot go without special authority (hyph) ....
 16 37 44 61 20 2 47 6

C. Snugly warm and comfortable .....
 50 4 64 13

D. Passionate; loving; enamored ....
 55 12 7 60 22 41 31

E. Delicate or pale color ....
 19 34 38 54

F. Roger ____ (in 1954 he became the first man to run a mile in under four minutes) ....
 24 18 8 36 25 43 32 51 11

G. Rate of walking, running, etc.; tempo; gait ....
 3 53 21 15

H. Comprehend; grasp the idea of ...
 56 46 39 59 33 42 63 10 26
 28

I. Radio's "___ and Andy" ....
 29 23 48 57

Y·E·A·R 1·9·7·6

	1 J	2 F	3 G	4 C	5 A		6 B	7 F	8 F	9 E	10 A	11 B
	12 D	13 E		14 H	15 F	16 J	17 A	18 F	19 B	20 C		21 F
22 I	23 B	24 A		25 H	26 F	27 C	28 B	29 F	30 A	31 F	32 I	33 B
34 I		35 A	36 F	37 F	38 C	39 H	40 F	41 J	42 A	43 D	44 E	45 A
46 G		47 F	48 H	49 A	50 G	51 H	52 C	53 D	54 H	55 A	56 F	

A. Raymond Burr has played this TV lawyer since 1957 (full name) ···
 __35__ __10__ __30__ __17__ __5__ __49__ __45__ __24__ __55__

 __42__

B. Meaning the opposite of what you seem to say or seem to mean .
 __19__ __11__ __28__ __23__ __33__ __6__

C. Rock group "The ____ and the Papas" ························
 __27__ __20__ __4__ __52__ __38__

D. Small child; add up ············
 __53__ __12__ __43__

E. ___ to be tied (informal; very annoyed or angry) ···············
 __13__ __44__ __9__

F. Scottish-born steel magnate/ philanthropist 1835-1919 (full name) ·························
 __7__ __47__ __40__ __36__ __26__ __21__ __29__ __31__ __8__

 __56__ __15__ __18__ __2__ __37__

G. .001 of an inch, used in measuring the diameter of wires .
 __3__ __50__ __46__

H. "Mood ____" (Duke Ellington composition) ···················
 __54__ __51__ __25__ __39__ __14__ __48__

I. Spasmodic, involuntary muscular contraction of the face ·········
 __32__ __22__ __34__

J. "Yankee Clipper" DiMaggio ·······
 __1__ __16__ __41__

25

Y·E·A·R 1·9·8·7

1 C	2 H	3 D		4 E	5 A	6 G	7 C	8 B		9 F	10 A	11 D	12 A
13 F	14 A	15 D	16 G	17 D	18 F	19 E		20 A	21 D	22 C	23 A	24 F	25 D
	26 E	27 B	28 A	29 C		30 G	31 A	32 B	33 G		34 D	35 D	36 C
37 H	38 D	39 A	40 D		41 F	42 D	43 F	44 C	45 D	46 H		47 A	48 D
	49 E	50 F	51 B	52 A	53 C		54 A	55 D	56 F	57 G	58 A	59 B	

A. First four words of a fairy tale
47 23 52 39 12 20 5 10 58
14 31 54 28

B. Intelligence; sense; understanding (slang) ....
8 51 32 27 59

C. Inebriated; tipsy; intoxicated ..
1 29 22 44 53 7 36

D. "_____ in Eighty Days" (3 wds; Jules Verne novel, 1873) ....
17 38 55 35 48 11 45 34 25
3 42 15 21 40

E. Posts of employment; duties; tasks; responsibilities ....
4 26 49 19

F. ____ the beans (informal; disclosing a secret) ....
13 41 9 18 50 43 56 24

G. Diabolically cruel or wicked person ....
30 16 33 6 57

H. Turf; surface of the ground .....
46 2 37

Y·E·A·R 1·4·6·B·C

1 F	2 A	3 F	4 E	5 D		6 F	7 C	8 G	9 B		10 G	11 C	12 A	13 A
	14 A	15 F	16 F	17 F	18 D		19 A	20 C	21 E	22 E		23 B	24 F	
25 F	26 A	27 C	28 C	29 B	30 D		31 A	32 C	33 B	34 F	35 A	36 D	37 G	38 H
	39 H	40 B		41 A	42 D	43 F		44 E	45 G	46 C	47 A	48 H	49 F	

A. Bugs Bunny's greeting (3 wds) ...

 __ __ __ __ __ __ __ __ __
 19 35 26 41 13 47 14 12 2

 __
 31

B. English poet Lord ____ (1788-1824), he wrote "She Walks in Beauty"

 __ __ __ __ __
 23 9 33 40 29

C. State bordered on the east by New Mexico and on the south by Mexico

 __ __ __ __ __ __ __
 20 7 28 27 46 11 32

D. US tennis star Michael

 __ __ __ __ __
 18 42 36 5 30

E. From ___ to riches (from extreme poverty to great wealth)

 __ __ __ __
 21 4 44 22

F. Pertaining to first principles; elementary; undeveloped; fundamental

 __ __ __ __ __ __ __ __ __
 25 15 49 17 3 43 16 34 6

 __ __
 1 24

G. Microorganism; microbe

 __ __ __ __
 37 10 45 8

H. Remainder after deducting charges, expenses, etc., from the gross

 __ __ __
 48 38 39

27

Y·E·A·R 1·9·4·4

	1 C	2 A	3 D	4 A	5 F		6 B	7 C	8 G	9 C		10 A	11 I
	12 B	13 C	14 J	15 A	16 H	17 H	18 A	19 B	20 C	21 A	22 E		23 A
24 B		25 D	26 I	27 H	28 A	29 F	30 G	31 J		32 A	33 H	34 I	35 I
36 A		37 F	38 H	39 J	40 A	41 D	42 H		43 F	44 D	45 A	46 E	47 G
48 D	49 I		50 C	51 A	52 D	53 A	54 F	55 F	56 A	57 E	58 A	59 B	

A. Dickens novel about the French Revolution (5 wds) ....
___ ___ ___ ___ ___ ___ ___ ___ ___
23 45 15 4   56 51 53 40 32

___ ___ ___ ___ ___ ___ ___
2   58 10 28 18 21 36

B. Harass; assail; surround ....
___ ___ ___ ___ ___
6   12 19 59 24

C. "Lizzie Borden took an axe/And gave her mother forty ___" ......
___ ___ ___ ___ ___ ___
1   20 7   50 9   13

D. "A ___ with the strange device, Excelsior!" (Longfellow, "Excelsior") ....
___ ___ ___ ___ ___ ___
25 44 48 52 41 3

E. Uproar; noisy clamor ....
___ ___ ___
22 46 57

F. ___ back (retraced one's footsteps) ....
___ ___ ___ ___ ___ ___
29 37 55 43 54 5

G. Mrs. John Lennon ....
___ ___ ___
47 8   30

H. Streep or Monroe hair color .....
___ ___ ___ ___ ___ ___
16 17 33 38 42 27

I. Refuse; waste product taken off molten metal during smelting ....
___ ___ ___ ___ ___
35 26 34 49 11

J. Its chemical symbol is Sn ....
___ ___ ___
14 39 31

28

Y·E·A·R 1·8·7·3

1 H	2 C	3 G	4 I	5 A	6 F	7 H	■	8 H	9 C	10 F	11 B	■
12 A	13 G	14 F	15 B	■	16 F	17 B	18 C	19 I	■	20 A	21 I	22 C
23 D	■	24 F	25 H	26 B	27 C	28 A	■	29 B	30 C	31 A	32 H	33 B
34 I	■	35 A	36 E	■	37 F	38 D	39 G	40 F	41 B	42 E	43 D	44 A
45 I	46 H	47 E	48 A	49 F	■	50 E	51 B	52 C	53 A	54 F	55 F	56 F

A. "It is the _____ that breaks the camel's back" (2 wds) ....
 $\overline{53}$ $\overline{5}$ $\overline{20}$ $\overline{35}$ $\overline{28}$ $\overline{44}$ $\overline{31}$ $\overline{48}$ $\overline{12}$

B. Prevent the occurrence of; make impossible ....
 $\overline{33}$ $\overline{41}$ $\overline{17}$ $\overline{51}$ $\overline{11}$ $\overline{26}$ $\overline{15}$ $\overline{29}$

C. Inquisitive; odd ....
 $\overline{52}$ $\overline{30}$ $\overline{27}$ $\overline{9}$ $\overline{22}$ $\overline{2}$ $\overline{18}$

D. Of a sickly pallor; ashen; lacking color ....
 $\overline{23}$ $\overline{43}$ $\overline{38}$

E. Soon; at once (archaic) ....
 $\overline{50}$ $\overline{42}$ $\overline{36}$ $\overline{47}$

F. He shot an apple off his son's head with bow and arrow (full name) ....
 $\overline{16}$ $\overline{55}$ $\overline{10}$ $\overline{49}$ $\overline{37}$ $\overline{54}$ $\overline{56}$ $\overline{24}$ $\overline{40}$
 $\overline{6}$ $\overline{14}$

G. Appropriate; suitable; proper; qualified ....
 $\overline{3}$ $\overline{13}$ $\overline{39}$

H. Silly mistake; blunder (slang; hyph) ....
 $\overline{1}$ $\overline{46}$ $\overline{7}$ $\overline{8}$ $\overline{32}$ $\overline{25}$

I. "Procrastination is the ___ of time" ....
 $\overline{19}$ $\overline{21}$ $\overline{45}$ $\overline{34}$ $\overline{4}$

Y·E·A·R 1·9·3·6

1 D	2 B	3 F	4 G	5 C	6 E		7 H	8 J	9 F	10 H	11 C	12 A	13 H
	14 G	15 I	16 C	17 I	18 A	19 F	20 H	21 J	22 D		23 G	24 E	
25 A	26 C	27 G	28 E		29 G	30 F	31 D		32 J	33 B	34 A	35 H	36 D
37 J	38 H		39 I	41 D	40 C	42 D	43 F		44 A	45 B		46 B	47 D
48 H	49 H	50 A	51 E	52 D	53 H	54 J		55 I	56 B	57 A	58 J	59 D	60 G

A. Arab emirate in the Persian Gulf

44 12 25 57 34 18 50

B. Walt Disney's cartoon dog ....

33 56 2 46 45

C. Group of twelve ....

5 26 11 40 16

D. Urge, provoke, incite ....

52 36 22 31 41 42 47 1 59

E. Virtuous; excellent; well-behaved ....

51 6 24 28

F. Brother of one's father or mother ....

30 19 9 3 43

G. Small room for storing clothing, food, etc. ....

14 27 29 60 4 23

H. Smallest continent ....

10 20 53 38 13 49 48 35 7

I. Antonym of "hard" ....

39 15 55 17

J. They're on the soles of the shoes of football or baseball players ....

58 8 21 32 54 37

30

Y·E·A·R 1·9·6·7

	1 D	2 G	3 A	4 C	5 B	6 D	7 F	8 A	9 I		10 G	11 H	12 A
13 F	14 H	15 E	16 I		17 A	18 D	19 I	20 C	21 H	22 F	23 E	24 A	25 F
26 G		27 C	28 F	29 G	30 A	31 A	32 F	33 B	34 G	35 E		36 A	37 B
38 A	39 C		40 F	41 C	42 A	43 H	44 I	45 F		46 A	47 F	48 C	49 B
50 E	51 F		52 F	53 C	54 A		55 D	56 C	57 A	58 F	59 G		

A. London's glass exhibition hall,
built in 1851 (2 wds) ....
$\overline{3}\ \overline{57}\ \overline{42}\ \overline{36}\ \overline{24}\ \overline{46}\ \overline{31}\ \overline{30}\ \overline{8}$
$\overline{38}\ \overline{12}\ \overline{17}\ \overline{54}$

B. Praise extravagantly; solicit
support for importunately ....
$\overline{5}\ \overline{37}\ \overline{49}\ \overline{33}$

C. "Chattanooga ____" (hyph; Glenn
Miller '40s song hit) ....
$\overline{20}\ \overline{4}\ \overline{41}\ \overline{48}\ \overline{27}\ \overline{53}\ \overline{56}\ \overline{39}$

D. The ___ and wherefores (cause
or reason) ....
$\overline{55}\ \overline{18}\ \overline{1}\ \overline{6}$

E. Transgressions of divine law ....
$\overline{23}\ \overline{15}\ \overline{50}\ \overline{35}$

F. Title song of a 1956 Elvis
Presley film (3 wds) ....
$\overline{58}\ \overline{28}\ \overline{40}\ \overline{45}\ \overline{7}\ \overline{22}\ \overline{52}\ \overline{32}\ \overline{13}$
$\overline{51}\ \overline{25}\ \overline{47}$

G. Incriminated an innocent person
through use of false evidence
(informal) ....
$\overline{10}\ \overline{26}\ \overline{2}\ \overline{29}\ \overline{34}\ \overline{59}$

H. Scorch ....
$\overline{14}\ \overline{21}\ \overline{43}\ \overline{11}$

I. "Of thee I ____" ....
$\overline{16}\ \overline{19}\ \overline{9}\ \overline{44}$

31

Y·E·A·R 1·9·8·1

	1 C	2 B	3 I	4 D		5 E	6 F	7 A		8 D	9 C	10 H
11 A	12 E	13 B	14 C	15 F		16 A	17 F		18 D	19 B	20 C	21 I
22 G	23 B		24 E	25 H	26 H	27 A	28 D	29 H	30 A		31 B	32 D
33 G	34 C	35 E	36 A	37 H		38 A	39 I	40 F	41 A		42 H	43 G
44 D	45 E	46 F		47 B	48 G	49 A	50 I	51 C	52 G	53 A	

A. "The ____" (part of James
Fenimore Cooper's series "The
Leatherstocking Tales") ....
 ‾7‾ ‾49‾ ‾36‾ ‾53‾ ‾30‾ ‾38‾ ‾16‾ ‾41‾ ‾11‾
 ‾27‾

B. Gloomy; sullen; moody ....
 ‾31‾ ‾13‾ ‾19‾ ‾2‾ ‾47‾ ‾23‾

C. "Kiss" was his 1986 hit single ..
 ‾1‾ ‾34‾ ‾20‾ ‾14‾ ‾51‾ ‾9‾

D. Creator of Li'l Abner, the
Shmoo, and Fearless Fosdick
(full name) ....
 ‾44‾ ‾28‾ ‾8‾ ‾32‾ ‾18‾ ‾4‾

E. Frenzied; agitated; frantic .....
 ‾12‾ ‾5‾ ‾45‾ ‾35‾ ‾24‾

F. Annie's pooch ....
 ‾17‾ ‾46‾ ‾6‾ ‾40‾ ‾15‾

G. Met soprano Leontyne ....
 ‾48‾ ‾33‾ ‾43‾ ‾22‾ ‾52‾

H. One of Santa's reindeer ....
 ‾42‾ ‾26‾ ‾37‾ ‾25‾ ‾29‾ ‾10‾

I. German novelist, author of "The
Magic Mountain" and "Death in
Venice" ....
 ‾3‾ ‾39‾ ‾50‾ ‾21‾

32

Y·E·A·R 1·9·8·7

1 D	2 A	3 F	4 E		5 C	6 A	7 G	8 C	9 H	10 A		11 B
12 G		13 E	14 F	15 D	16 H	17 E	18 D	19 D		20 B	21 A	22 F
23 D	24 B	25 G		26 I	27 B	28 A	29 C		30 I	31 H	32 B	
33 G	34 E	35 G	36 A		37 B	38 A	39 C	40 D	41 I	42 A	43 B	44 G
45 B	46 C		47 F	48 F		49 A	50 I	51 B	52 E	53 G	54 B	

A. Ancient amphitheater of Rome ···· $\overline{49}$ $\overline{38}$ $\overline{28}$ $\overline{2}$ $\overline{42}$ $\overline{10}$ $\overline{6}$ $\overline{21}$ $\overline{36}$

B. Fred, Wilma, or Pebbles ········ $\overline{37}$ $\overline{51}$ $\overline{27}$ $\overline{45}$ $\overline{20}$ $\overline{54}$ $\overline{43}$ $\overline{11}$ $\overline{32}$

$\overline{24}$

C. Written or published defamatory statement ······················· $\overline{29}$ $\overline{8}$ $\overline{5}$ $\overline{46}$ $\overline{39}$

D. German engineer (1902-1988), inventor of the rotary internal combustion engine ··············· $\overline{1}$ $\overline{15}$ $\overline{23}$ $\overline{40}$ $\overline{18}$ $\overline{19}$

E. Lever for imparting rotary motion; tool needed to start early motor cars ················ $\overline{13}$ $\overline{34}$ $\overline{52}$ $\overline{17}$ $\overline{4}$

F. Direction to the left of a person facing the rising sun ···· $\overline{22}$ $\overline{48}$ $\overline{3}$ $\overline{47}$ $\overline{14}$

G. ____ around (wasting time) ······ $\overline{33}$ $\overline{44}$ $\overline{35}$ $\overline{25}$ $\overline{53}$ $\overline{12}$ $\overline{7}$

H. She lives in a convent ·········· $\overline{9}$ $\overline{31}$ $\overline{16}$

I. "... said Simple Simon to the pie man, let me taste your ____" $\overline{26}$ $\overline{50}$ $\overline{30}$ $\overline{41}$

33

Y·E·A·R B·I·B·L·I·C·A·L

	1 J	2 B	3 J	4 A	5 C	6 B	7 B		8 C	9 A	10 B	11 C	12 F
13 F	14 D	15 E	16 B		17 C	18 B	19 I		20 A	21 D		22 C	23 B	24 F
	25 F	26 A	27 B	28 B	29 H		30 G	31 H	32 A	33 C		34 F	35 E	36 D
	37 B	38 G	39 H	.	40 F	41 B	42 J	43 H		44 B	45 H	46 C		47 I
48 F	49 J	50 J	51 B	52 J	53 H	54 D		55 F	56 I	57 G	58 C		59 A	60 B
61 J	62 D	63 A	64 E		65 J	66 H		67 B	68 I	69 A	70 C			

A. He carved Pinocchio ....
‾59 ‾69 ‾26 ‾4 ‾63 ‾32 ‾20 ‾9

B. "O, what a rogue ____ am I," says Hamlet (3 wds) ....,.........
‾23 ‾6 ‾41 ‾27 ‾67 ‾37 ‾51 ‾60 ‾10
‾7 ‾16 ‾28 ‾44 ‾18 ‾2

C. Ardor; fervor; vigorous impetuosity; fury ....
‾11 ‾5 ‾33 ‾22 ‾58 ‾17 ‾70 ‾8 ‾46

D. Translated into a computer language ....
‾14 ‾21 ‾54 ‾36 ‾62

E. "A ____ is only an egg's way of making another egg" (Samuel Butler, 1835-1902) ....
‾35 ‾15 ‾64

F. Walt Disney's animated film version of great musical works ..
‾55 ‾40 ‾13 ‾24 ‾48 ‾34 ‾12 ‾25

G. "Good" in Paris ....
‾30 ‾57 ‾38

H. "From every mountainside/ Let ____ ring" ....
‾66 ‾45 ‾29 ‾53 ‾39 ‾31 ‾43

I. Procreated; brought up; reared ..
‾47 ‾56 ‾19 ‾68

J. George of the Beatles ....
‾52 ‾42 ‾61 ‾3 ‾50 ‾1 ‾65 ‾49

Y·E·A·R 1·9·4·5

	1 A	2 B	3 C	4 B	5 F		6 D	7 A	8 E	9 F	10 B	11 G	12 E
13 A	14 D	15 I		16 B	17 B	18 G	19 F	20 E	21 B	22 G	23 G	24 D	25 C
26 A	27 G	28 E	29 B	30 C		31 G	32 C	33 G	34 B	35 E		36 H	37 G
38 B	39 G	40 H		41 C	42 E	43 B	44 G	45 C		46 E	47 B		48 D
49 H	50 I	51 E	52 I	53 I	54 G	55 B		56 G	57 G		58 E	59 A	60 I
61 G	62 B	63 I	64 C		65 C	66 G	67 E	68 D	69 C	70 A	71 I	72 D	

A. Seaport capital of Alaska .... ___ ___ ___ ___ ___ ___
1 7 26 13 59 70

B. "Yond' Cassius has a ____ look"
(3 wds; "Julius Caesar" I, ii) .. ___ ___ ___ ___ ___ ___ ___ ___ ___
29 10 4 17 2 47 21 62 16

___ ___ ___ ___
34 38 43 55

C. Ostentatious display of
importance .... ___ ___ ___ ___ ___ ___ ___ ___ ___
3 25 65 64 69 45 32 41 30

D. Turning point .... ___ ___ ___ ___ ___ ___
48 14 72 68 24 6

E. Uncultivated region, as of
forest or desert .... ___ ___ ___ ___ ___ ___ ___ ___ ___
58 46 28 12 42 8 20 51 67

___
35

F. Used in negative phrases,
especially after "neither" ...... ___ ___ ___
5 19 9

G. Term describing soldiers
unaccounted for after a battle
(3 wds) .... ___ ___ ___ ___ ___ ___ ___ ___ ___
44 66 31 61 22 11 33 37 54

___ ___ ___ ___ ___ ___
27 18 23 39 56 57

H. Paint the town ___ (celebrate
boisterously) .... ___ ___ ___
36 49 40

I. Gives a faithful
representation, image, or idea
of .... ___ ___ ___ ___ ___ ___ ___
52 63 71 60 53 50 15

35

Y·E·A·R 1·9·5·4

1 A	2 C	3 D	4 H	5 A	6 A	7 H		8 B	9 H	10 F	11 H	12 D
13 A	14 I	15 B	16 B	17 H		18 A	19 C	20 E	21 H		22 B	23 F	24 A	25 D
26 E	27 F	28 G	29 B		30 I	31 A	32 F		33 B	34 H	35 I	36 H	37 H
38 F	39 G	40 E	41 F	42 C	43 B		44 A	45 C	46 H	47 H	48 I	49 A	50 C	51 B
52 G		53 G	54 D	55 H		56 C	57 C	58 A	59 D	60 B	61 F	62 H	

A. Miss Piggy, Kermit, and the
rest of the gang (2 wds) .... ── ── ── ── ── ── ── ── ──
49 13 5 6 31 24 58 44 18

── 1

B. Came together as one; fused;
united .... ── ── ── ── ── ── ── ── ──
8 51 60 15 29 22 43 33 16

C. US magician and escape artist,
1874-1926 .... ── ── ── ── ── ── ──
19 57 2 45 50 56 42

D. Rio de la ___ (estuary between
Argentina and Uruguay) .... ── ── ── ── ──
3 59 54 12 25

E. Legal profession .... ── ── ──
40 20 26

F. Juliet's family name .... ── ── ── ── ── ── ──
61 27 38 10 41 23 32

G. Search for; seek; endeavor to
find .... ── ── ── ──
53 39 52 28

H. Small, cramped place (2 wds) .... ── ── ── ── ── ── ── ── ──
47 37 9 17 62 34 46 36 4

── ── ── ──
21 7 11 55

I. "___ Ben Adhem (may his tribe
increase!)/Awoke one night from
a deep dream of peace" (Hunt) ... ── ── ── ──
48 30 14 35

36

Y·E·A·R 1·9·6·5

	1 D	2 F	3 K	4 A	5 C	6 F		7 E	8 K	9 C	10 I	11 I	12 H
	13 B	14 G	15 A	16 J		17 E	18 K	19 B	20 F	21 I		22 L	23 C
24 H	25 I	26 C	■		27 G	28 B	29 A	30 H	31 F	32 I		33 D	34 B	35 L
36 E	37 K	■		38 B	39 G	40 C	41 L	42 D	43 I	44 H		45 G	46 L	
47 J	48 B	49 A	50 K	51 J	52 G		53 I	54 D	55 F	56 B		57 C	58 D
59 C	60 F		61 E	62 C	63 D		64 G	65 K	66 E	67 I	68 A		

A. Mrs. Ronald Reagan .... __ __ __ __ __
4 49 68 29 15

B. You can't make these without
breaking some eggs .... __ __ __ __ __ __ __
34 13 48 19 28 38 56

C. Quality of being modest .... __ __ __ __ __ __ __ __
57 62 59 23 9 40 5 26

D. Studying with steady attention .. __ __ __ __ __ __
42 58 33 54 63 1

E. All-time leading rusher in NFL
history (1957-65) .... __ __ __ __ __
17 61 66 7 36

F. Agassi and Capriati's game ...... __ __ __ __ __ __
20 60 31 55 2 6

G. Great oaks from little ____ grow __ __ __ __ __ __
14 64 45 39 52 27

H. Golfers' cry .... __ __ __ __
24 30 44 12

I. US frontier region in the 19th
century (2 wds) .... __ __ __ __ __ __ __ __
53 11 10 32 67 43 21 25

J. International distress call ..... __ __ __
16 51 47

K. Lifted up; elevated .... __ __ __ __ __ __
65 3 8 50 18 37

L. The Magic Dragon .... __ __ __ __
41 35 22 46

37

Y·E·A·R 1·9·3·5

		1 G	2 C	3 D	4 A	5 I	6 B		7 H	8 C	9 K	10 B	11 H
12 C		13 J	14 B	15 F		16 C	17 D	18 D	19 I	20 E	21 B	22 D	
23 E	24 J	25 D	26 F	27 J	28 E	29 A	30 B		31 G	32 C	33 I	34 E	35 G
	36 I	37 G		38 A	39 D	40 E	41 I	42 I	43 C		44 F	45 G	46 E
47 J	48 I		49 F	50 B	51 C	52 I	53 H	54 F	55 K		56 A	57 J	58 D
59 B	60 A		61 I	62 C	63 B		64 K	65 D	66 C	67 J			

A. "When you call me that, ___"
(Owen Wister 1860-1938, "The
Virginian") ....
60 56 4 29 38

B. Jonathan Swift's traveler to
Brobdingnag ....
6 50 21 30 14 10 59 63

C. Woman without a husband; man
without a wife ....
66 51 16 2 8 12 32 62 43

D. Black Muslim leader,
assassinated in NYC in 1965;
title character of 1992 film ....
25 17 58 3 65 18 22 39

E. Most popular sport in the world .
34 20 40 23 28 46

F. SW Australian port on the
Indian Ocean ....
26 54 15 44 49

G. Foam; spume ....
31 1 37 35 45

H. Radically left politically;
communist ....
53 11 7

I. Earlier example or a prior
legal decision ....
61 33 48 19 42 52 41 5 36

J. Belgrade is the capital of this
Balkan state ....
13 47 67 27 57 24

K. Concealed from sight; covered up
64 9 55

Y·E·A·R 1·9·3·9

	1 A	2 E	3 B	4 C		5 J	6 E	7 A	8 A	9 C	10 I	
	11 H	12 F	13 E	14 K	15 A	16 F	17 C	18 A	19 H	20 F		
21 E	22 E	23 K	24 I		25 B	26 F	27 H	28 A		29 I	30 J	
31 E	32 L	33 H		34 A	35 E	36 D	37 L		38 E	39 B	40 J	
41 G	42 E	43 L	44 A	45 F	46 K	47 E		48 D	49 C	50 J	51 A	
52 E	53 L		54 B	55 G	56 A	57 E	58 B		59 C	60 L	61 G	
62 A	63 I	64 J		65 C	66 A		67 K	68 A	69 G	70 H	71 A	
	72 L	73 D		74 D	75 A	76 E	77 D	78 J	79 B	80 F	81 A	

A. Mrs. Billy Joel (full name) ..... $\overline{7}$ $\overline{18}$ $\overline{75}$ $\overline{34}$ $\overline{81}$ $\overline{56}$ $\overline{44}$ $\overline{28}$ $\overline{51}$

$\overline{68}$ $\overline{71}$ $\overline{1}$ $\overline{8}$ $\overline{15}$ $\overline{62}$ $\overline{66}$

B. N Atlantic islands 800 miles west of Portugal .... $\overline{54}$ $\overline{3}$ $\overline{39}$ $\overline{58}$ $\overline{79}$ $\overline{25}$

C. Having a preconceived opinion; showing prejudice .... $\overline{65}$ $\overline{4}$ $\overline{49}$ $\overline{17}$ $\overline{9}$ $\overline{59}$

D. "____ your wagon to a star" (Emerson) .... $\overline{48}$ $\overline{77}$ $\overline{36}$ $\overline{74}$ $\overline{73}$

E. Juliet Capulet loves _____ (full name) .... $\overline{22}$ $\overline{52}$ $\overline{31}$ $\overline{42}$ $\overline{6}$ $\overline{38}$ $\overline{47}$ $\overline{35}$ $\overline{13}$

$\overline{2}$ $\overline{21}$ $\overline{76}$ $\overline{57}$

F. Neat; trim; smart .... $\overline{45}$ $\overline{12}$ $\overline{26}$ $\overline{20}$ $\overline{16}$ $\overline{80}$

G. Petty quarrel .... $\overline{41}$ $\overline{69}$ $\overline{55}$ $\overline{61}$

H. "... but when a man ___ a dog that is news" (Charles Dana) .... $\overline{11}$ $\overline{19}$ $\overline{70}$ $\overline{27}$ $\overline{33}$

I. Horizontally level .... $\overline{24}$ $\overline{29}$ $\overline{63}$ $\overline{10}$

J. Short race at full speed .... $\overline{78}$ $\overline{5}$ $\overline{50}$ $\overline{30}$ $\overline{40}$ $\overline{64}$

K. Moderate or restrain; diminish .. $\overline{67}$ $\overline{23}$ $\overline{14}$ $\overline{46}$

L. Confirms, substantiates, verifies .... $\overline{32}$ $\overline{53}$ $\overline{37}$ $\overline{43}$ $\overline{60}$ $\overline{72}$

Y·E·A·R B·I·B·L·I·C·A·L

		1 K	2 I	3 J	4 B	5 A	6 I		7 F	8 A	9 B	10 A	11 I
	12 B	13 D	14 A	15 E	16 G	17 A	18 J	19 B	20 C	21 J		22 I	23 D
24 I	25 H	26 A		27 K	28 J	29 I	30 B	31 J		32 E	33 C	34 A	35 I
36 F	37 H		38 D	39 A	40 J	41 I		42 D	43 K	44 C	45 I	46 B	47 H
48 D	49 E	50 C	51 F		52 C	53 B	54 I	55 A	56 G		57 C	58 H	59 K
60 K	61 B	62 A	63 E		64 C	65 B	66 J		67 E	68 A	69 I	70 G	
71 J	72 H	73 J		74 A	75 F	76 D		77 G	78 B	79 A	80 C	

A. Its state capital is Columbia
(2 wds) ....
___ ___ ___ ___ ___ ___ ___ ___ ___
26 34 68 62 74 14 79 17 39
___ ___ ___ ___
5   10 55 8

B. Describing a person who
introduced something new or
imaginative ....
___ ___ ___ ___ ___ ___ ___ ___ ___
53 30 65 19 12 61 4   46 9
___
78

C. "You're a better man than I am,
___!" (2 wds; from a poem by
Kipling) ....
___ ___ ___ ___ ___ ___ ___ ___
57 20 50 52 64 80 44 33

D. Slow-thinking; dull; foolish ....
___ ___ ___ ___ ___ ___
76 48 23 42 13 38

E. Through ___ and thin
(steadfastly) ....
___ ___ ___ ___ ___
15 63 49 67 32

F. The little Dutch boy put his
finger in the ____ ....
___ ___ ___ ___
7   75 36 51

G. Multitude of persons or things ..
___ ___ ___ ___
77 16 70 56

H. "The Mill on the ____" (1860
novel by George Eliot) ....
___ ___ ___ ___ ___
72 25 58 47 37

I. Disinfected water by adding a
certain chemical ....
___ ___ ___ ___ ___ ___ ___ ___ ___
35 22 45 29 24 2   41 54 69
___ ___
6   11

J. A ____ drinker (hyph; using
both hands) ....
___ ___ ___ ___ ___ ___ ___ ___ ___
28 40 71 73 18 21 3   31 66

K. "The ___ are alive with the
sound of music" ....
___ ___ ___ ___ ___
43 60 1   59 27

40

Y·E·A·R 1·5·8·8

1 H	2 I	3 C	4 G	5 E	6 A	7 D	8 I	9 F	10 B		11 E	12 D
13 A	14 G	15 E	16 G	17 B		18 I	19 A	20 A	21 B	22 E	23 A	
24 B	25 J	26 B	27 F	28 E	29 D		30 B	31 J	32 J		33 H	34 A
	35 E	36 D	37 G	38 I	39 F	40 B	41 G		42 G	43 B	44 I	45 A
46 D		47 E	48 C	49 A	50 F	51 H		52 A	53 B	54 E	55 I	56 C
	57 A	58 G	59 B		60 I	61 A	62 A	63 J	64 C	65 B	66 A	

A. Oscars (2 wds) .... $\overline{61}$ $\overline{6}$ $\overline{13}$ $\overline{52}$ $\overline{45}$ $\overline{20}$ $\overline{34}$ $\overline{57}$ $\overline{62}$

$\overline{23}$ $\overline{19}$ $\overline{49}$ $\overline{66}$

B. Smallest US state (2 wds) .... $\overline{53}$ $\overline{17}$ $\overline{30}$ $\overline{59}$ $\overline{10}$ $\overline{26}$ $\overline{40}$ $\overline{43}$ $\overline{21}$

$\overline{65}$ $\overline{24}$

C. Plant having a long, slender
stem that trails on the ground .. $\overline{3}$ $\overline{64}$ $\overline{48}$ $\overline{56}$

D. Out of ____ (no longer
available from the publisher) ... $\overline{12}$ $\overline{36}$ $\overline{7}$ $\overline{29}$ $\overline{46}$

E. Unprejudiced; impartial .... $\overline{47}$ $\overline{5}$ $\overline{35}$ $\overline{15}$ $\overline{54}$ $\overline{11}$ $\overline{28}$ $\overline{22}$

F. Wicked; nefarious .... $\overline{50}$ $\overline{27}$ $\overline{39}$ $\overline{9}$

G. Scandinavian language related
to Hungarian .... $\overline{42}$ $\overline{4}$ $\overline{58}$ $\overline{14}$ $\overline{37}$ $\overline{16}$ $\overline{41}$

H. Eve was created from Adam's ___ . $\overline{51}$ $\overline{1}$ $\overline{33}$

I. "I cried all the way to ___"
(2 wds; Liberace) .... $\overline{38}$ $\overline{60}$ $\overline{44}$ $\overline{8}$ $\overline{18}$ $\overline{2}$ $\overline{55}$

J. Native of Ankara .... $\overline{32}$ $\overline{31}$ $\overline{25}$ $\overline{63}$

41

Y·E·A·R 1·8·1·2

1 A	2 E	3 H	4 G	5 A	6 B	7 F	8 C	■	9 A	10 H	11 B	12 G
13 E	■	14 E	15 B	16 B	17 C	18 G	19 D	20 G	■	21 H	22 B	23 D
24 I	■	25 A	26 C	27 B	28 E	29 F	30 A	31 A	■	32 G	33 D	34 D
35 A	36 I	37 G	38 B	39 C	■	40 A	41 D	42 F	43 H	44 B	45 I	46 C
47 I	■	48 F	49 B	■	50 A	51 G	52 I	53 I	54 B	55 A	56 D	57 C

A. 1980 film that won DeNiro best actor Oscar as fighter Jake LaMotta (2 wds) ....
$\overline{40}\ \overline{30}\ \overline{9}\ \overline{55}\ \overline{1}\ \overline{25}\ \overline{50}\ \overline{35}\ \overline{5}$
$\overline{31}$

B. Inclined to seek revenge ....
$\overline{38}\ \overline{44}\ \overline{27}\ \overline{54}\ \overline{15}\ \overline{16}\ \overline{49}\ \overline{11}\ \overline{22}$
$\overline{6}$

C. "I could write a ___ about your Easter bonnet" (Irving Berlin) ..
$\overline{39}\ \overline{57}\ \overline{8}\ \overline{46}\ \overline{26}\ \overline{17}$

D. False; incorrect; unfaithful ....
$\overline{41}\ \overline{56}\ \overline{34}\ \overline{19}\ \overline{33}\ \overline{23}$

E. Rescue from danger; stop a hockey puck from entering one's goal ....
$\overline{13}\ \overline{2}\ \overline{14}\ \overline{28}$

F. ___ Bonheur (1822-1899; French animal painter, famous for "The Horse Fair") ....
$\overline{29}\ \overline{7}\ \overline{42}\ \overline{48}$

G. Mrs. John Lennon (full name) ....
$\overline{20}\ \overline{51}\ \overline{32}\ \overline{4}\ \overline{37}\ \overline{12}\ \overline{18}$

H. ___ opera (daytime TV melodrama)
$\overline{43}\ \overline{21}\ \overline{10}\ \overline{3}$

I. "The ____ Edge" (1944 Somerset Maugham novel) ....
$\overline{24}\ \overline{45}\ \overline{36}\ \overline{53}\ \overline{52}\ \overline{47}$

42

Y·E·A·R 1·9·0·1

	1 J	2 F	3 A	4 I	5 B	6 J	7 A	8 D		9 J
10 F		11 B	12 I	13 C	14 A	15 D	16 F	17 B	18 A	19 J	20 C
21 B	22 K		23 A	24 E		25 A	26 H	27 J	28 A	29 H	30 A
31 F	32 E	33 A		34 J	35 A	36 H	37 C	38 C	39 F	40 A	41 H
	42 F	43 G	44 K	45 F	46 A	47 K	48 G	49 B	50 H		51 F
52 A	53 B	54 J	55 K	56 E	57 H	58 C		59 G	60 D		61 A
62 F	63 E	64 I	65 A	66 B	67 C	68 A	69 F	70 J		

A. She won Oscars for "The Lion in
Winter," "On Golden Pond," and
two other films (full name) .....
___ ___ ___ ___ ___ ___ ___ ___ ___
 3   25   33   30   14   40   65   18   46

___ ___ ___ ___ ___ ___ ___
35   7   61   23   52   28   68

B. Its capital city is Reykjavik ...
___ ___ ___ ___ ___ ___ ___
17   53   21   49   11   5   66

C. Mixed a salad lightly and
gently to coat the ingredients
with the dressing ....
___ ___ ___ ___ ___ ___
20   37   13   58   67   38

D. Salty sauce much used on dishes
in the Orient ....
___ ___ ___
15   60   8

E. "Night hath a thousand ___"
(Lyly, "Maides Metamorphosis") ..
___ ___ ___ ___
56   24   63   32

F. Having many intersecting lines;
tick-tack-toe ....
___ ___ ___ ___ ___ ___ ___ ___ ___
69   62   31   45   51   2   42   39   10

___
16

G. One of the ten little piggies ...
___ ___ ___
59   43   48

H. Appropriate; respectable; proper
___ ___ ___ ___ ___ ___
57   41   29   36   26   50

I. Your mother's daughter
(informal) ....
___ ___ ___
12   4   64

J. ___ Jane (1870s Deadwood, South
Dakota gal, Wild Bill Hickock's
mistress) ....
___ ___ ___ ___ ___ ___ ___ ___
54   27   6   19   1   9   34   70

K. Symbol of peace ....
___ ___ ___ ___
22   44   47   55

43

Y·E·A·R 1·9·7·9

	1 B	2 F	3 G	4 H	5 F	6 C	7 B	8 F	9 E		10 F	11 F	12 C	13 F
14 B		15 F	16 C	17 D		18 F	19 A	20 B	21 F	22 D		23 A	24 B	25 F
26 C	27 A	28 B	29 G	30 F		31 E	32 A	33 A	34 F	35 F		36 G	37 F	38 C
39 A		40 B	41 F	42 H	43 F	44 B		45 A	46 B	47 E	48 C	49 G	50 D	
51 A	52 D		53 B	54 F	55 H	56 C		57 D	58 B	59 G	60 A	61 G	

A. "O'er the ramparts we watched were so gallantly ____ " (Francis Scott Key) ....
$\overline{27}\ \overline{45}\ \overline{19}\ \overline{32}\ \overline{51}\ \overline{23}\ \overline{60}\ \overline{39}\ \overline{33}$

B. Hasten the occurrence of; bring about suddenly; reckless ....
$\overline{1}\ \overline{46}\ \overline{7}\ \overline{53}\ \overline{20}\ \overline{40}\ \overline{24}\ \overline{14}\ \overline{58}$
$\overline{28}\ \overline{44}$

C. Unnecessary verbiage used deliberately to lengthen a speech ....
$\overline{56}\ \overline{48}\ \overline{6}\ \overline{12}\ \overline{26}\ \overline{16}\ \overline{38}$

D. Jack, Joe, Bobby and ____ ......
$\overline{52}\ \overline{22}\ \overline{57}\ \overline{17}\ \overline{50}$

E. Lay a wager ....
$\overline{31}\ \overline{47}\ \overline{9}$

F. Gershwin 1928 orchestral piece; Gene Kelly/Leslie Caron 1951 musical film (4 wds) ....
$\overline{15}\ \overline{35}\ \overline{11}\ \overline{21}\ \overline{41}\ \overline{2}\ \overline{5}\ \overline{43}\ \overline{54}$
$\overline{25}\ \overline{34}\ \overline{8}\ \overline{18}\ \overline{13}\ \overline{30}\ \overline{37}\ \overline{10}$

G. Held permanently and inalienably; protected by law or ownership ....
$\overline{59}\ \overline{3}\ \overline{36}\ \overline{49}\ \overline{29}\ \overline{61}$

H. Surface-to-air missile ....
$\overline{4}\ \overline{42}\ \overline{55}$

44

Y·E·A·R 1·4·5·3

■	1 A	2 D	3 F	4 G	5 A	6 H	7 F	■	8 B	9 A	10 D	11 G
12 H	13 A	14 E	15 B	16 A	■	17 A	18 A	19 A	20 H	21 C	22 F	■	23 G
24 A	25 A	26 C	27 C	■	28 B	29 G	■	30 A	31 E	32 B	■	33 D	34 C
35 A	36 B	37 D	■	38 A	39 C	40 B	41 E	42 D	43 A	44 C	■	45 C	46 G
47 F	48 A	49 F	50 H	51 B	52 D	53 A	54 E	55 F	56 A	57 A	58 A	■

A. Baroness Orczy's elusive French revolution hero (3 wds) ....

  30 9 17 48 38 24 43 57 1

  13 19 53 18 56 5 35 16

  58 25

B. Flapjack ....

  40 15 51 8 28 36 32

C. Pertaining to worldly things, or to things not regarded as religious or spiritual ....

  27 44 45 34 26 39 21

D. Gilbert ___ (1755–1828; artist famous for his portrait of George Washington) ....

  37 52 42 2 10 33

E. Indirect suggestion; innuendo; inkling ....

  31 14 54 41

F. Lyric poem of 14 lines, usually in iambic pentameter, with an intricate rhyme scheme ....

  3 55 47 7 22 49

G. Force upon or impose fraudulently or unjustifiably ...

  23 46 11 29 4

H. Garment worn by Hindu women .....

  12 50 6 20

45

Y·E·A·R 1·7·5·5

	1 G	2 G	3 H	4 B	5 E	6 G	7 A		8 A	9 B	10 G	11 D
12 E	13 A	14 I	15 G		16 H	17 B		18 A	19 I	20 C	21 E	22 A
23 A	24 I		25 G	26 C	27 C	28 F	29 H	30 B	31 D		32 G	33 I
	34 A	35 C	36 D	37 E	38 B	39 F		40 A	41 I	42 D	♡	43 E
44 G	45 F	46 A	47 D	48 G		49 F	50 H	51 A	52 A	53 A	54 B	

A. Upstate NY AFL team, loser in
1991 Super Bowl (2 wds) ·········
___ ___ ___ ___ ___ ___ ___ ___ ___
8 52 18 34 40 22 13 51 46

___ ___ ___
23   7 53

B. Sam and Diane used to steam up
the beer steins at this bar ·····
___ ___ ___ ___ ___ ___
38 54 30   4   9 17

C. Defeat attended with disorderly
flight; overwhelm; subdue ·······
___ ___ ___ ___
35 26 27 20

D. Calculated the sum of; said or
wrote further; appended ·········
___ ___ ___ ___ ___
47 31 11 36 42

E. Go down the ___ (become
worthless) ·····················
___ ___ ___ ___ ___
12   5 21 43 37

F. With a heavy ____ (with
severity; oppressively;
awkwardly) ·····················
___ ___ ___ ___
39 49 28 45

G. Realization or coming into
awareness of something ·········
___ ___ ___ ___ ___ ___ ___ ___ ___
10 25   6 15   2 44 32 48   1

H. Keep in ____ (remember) ·········
___ ___ ___ ___
50 16   3 29

I. Astute; shrewd; sagacious ·······
___ ___ ___ ___ ___
14 19 41 33 24

46

Y·E·A·R 1·7·8·9

	1 E	2 A	3 C	4 A	5 B	6 F	7 H	8 D	9 B		10 A	11 H
12 G	13 B		14 A	15 A	16 C	17 E		18 D	19 F	20 A	21 B	22 C	23 A
24 A		25 D	26 A	27 B	28 A		29 G	30 G	31 E	32 A	33 E	34 E	
35 G	36 G	37 A	38 F	39 E	40 C	41 E		42 G	43 B	44 F	45 A	46 C	
47 E	48 B	49 A		50 B	51 H	52 E	53 A	54 G	55 B		56 D	57 E	58 A
	59 C	60 D	61 B		62 G	63 G	64 E	65 D	66 B	67 A			

A. Dying words of the commander of the frigate Chesapeake, 1813 (5 wds) ....
 49 14 32 10 45 20 15 58 2
 37 67 26 53 23 24 4 28

B. Cave-dwelling TV cartoon family, 1960-66 ....
 66 43 27 5 61 55 21 50 48
 13 9

C. Member of one of the two great religious divisions of Islam ....
 59 46 22 40 3 16

D. Sauté in fat and then cook slowly in very little liquid ....
 18 8 56 65 25 60

E. Haberdasher who became president of the US (full name) .
 52 39 57 64 34 33 17 31 1
 47 41

F. Make weary; become fatigued; bore ....
 38 44 19 6

G. It's behind the basketball hoop .
 29 36 35 12 42 30 62 54 63

H. Consumed food; wore away; corroded ....
 11 51 7

47

Y·E·A·R 1·8·1·4

	1 F	2 A	3 C	4 B	5 D		6 E	7 A	8 C	9 A	10 A	11 A	12 H	13 E
	14 E	15 B	16 C		17 G	18 E	19 A	20 C	21 E		22 F	23 G	24 F	25 G
26 B	27 H	28 H		29 A	30 D	31 B	32 A	33 E	34 H		35 H	36 A		37 A
38 A	39 B	40 A	41 F	42 E	43 A	44 A	45 D		46 B	47 G	48 E	49 C	

A. From ____ (3 wds; slang: on good authority; from a trustworthy source) .... $\overline{32}$ $\overline{37}$ $\overline{19}$ $\overline{2}$ $\overline{44}$ $\overline{29}$ $\overline{11}$ $\overline{7}$ $\overline{40}$

$\overline{10}$ $\overline{38}$ $\overline{9}$ $\overline{36}$ $\overline{43}$

B. Poised; sophisticated; refined .. $\overline{31}$ $\overline{39}$ $\overline{46}$ $\overline{26}$ $\overline{15}$ $\overline{4}$

C. ___ vegetables have been cut into small cubes .... $\overline{16}$ $\overline{3}$ $\overline{8}$ $\overline{20}$ $\overline{49}$

D. Who goes there? Friend or ___? .. $\overline{5}$ $\overline{30}$ $\overline{45}$

E. "For ____ was a boojum, you see" (2 wds; from a poem by Lewis Carroll) .... $\overline{6}$ $\overline{13}$ $\overline{33}$ $\overline{42}$ $\overline{48}$ $\overline{14}$ $\overline{18}$ $\overline{21}$

F. They're rolled in Monopoly, Trivial Pursuit, and Craps ...... $\overline{24}$ $\overline{22}$ $\overline{1}$ $\overline{41}$

G. French Riviera city .... $\overline{23}$ $\overline{25}$ $\overline{17}$ $\overline{47}$

H. Natives of Copenhagen .... $\overline{34}$ $\overline{35}$ $\overline{27}$ $\overline{12}$ $\overline{28}$

48

Y·E·A·R 1·9·4·0

1 H	2 B	3 C	4 A	5 F		6 G	7 A	8 D	9 A		10 A	11 C
12 E		13 D	14 A	15 F	16 A	17 C	18 A	19 F	20 G	21 E	22 B	
23 A	24 F		25 A	26 B	27 H	28 G		29 A	30 C	31 F	32 A	33 A
34 A	35 E	36 D	37 G	38 A		39 H	40 B		41 C	42 A	43 A	44 A
45 D	46 A		47 B	48 E	49 C	50 D	51 A	52 H	53 E	54 F	55 C	

A. Song from "Porgy and Bess" says this about "things that you're liable to read in the Bible" (4 wds) ....
42 14 33 23 38 18 43 9 34
51 4 25 29 32 16 10 46
44 7

B. Miss Boop ....
47 22 26 40 2

C. Acquire or appropriate before someone else; usurp ....
17 49 11 55 41 3 30

D. Blouse and peaked cap, considered together, worn by a jockey ....
8 36 50 45 13

E. Adventurous search by a knight (as by Don Quixote) ....
53 48 12 21 35

F. Pledge, guaranty, or bond; certainty ....
24 54 15 19 31 5

G. Cry of the lion ....
28 37 20 6

H. Any legend of heroic exploits ...
52 27 1 39

49

Y·E·A·R 1·9·4·9

	1 B	2 A	3 D	4 G	5 B	6 E		7 C	8 I	9 H	▬	10 F	11 B
12 A	13 E		14 F	15 H	16 A		17 B	18 A	19 F		20 G	21 H	22 A
23 D	24 G	25 A	26 E		27 C	28 G	29 B	30 G	31 G	32 A	33 C	34 B	35 A
36 G		37 I	38 G	39 A	40 A		41 H	42 D	43 I	44 C	45 I	46 A	47 B
48 D		49 H	50 C	51 H		52 A	53 B	54 E	55 A	56 D	57 G		

A. Single by USA for Africa; 1985 best record Grammy (4 wds) ......
 ___ ___ ___ ___ ___ ___ ___ ___ ___
 18 40 46 32 12 52 2   39 55

 ___ ___ ___ ___
 25 35 22 16

B. Strong inclination, taste, or liking for something ....
 ___ ___ ___ ___ ___ ___ ___ ___
 29 34 5   1   11 53 47 17

C. Overhand, figure of eight, slip, square and clove hitch ....
 ___ ___ ___ ___ ___
 7   44 50 33 27

D. ___ Lama (former ruler and chief monk of Tibet) ....
 ___ ___ ___ ___ ___
 48 42 23 56 3

E. Billie Jean ___ (6-time Wimbledon champion and 4-time US Open winner) ....
 ___ ___ ___ ___
 13 54 26 6

F. ___ Paolo (Brazil's largest city) ....
 ___ ___ ___
 10 14 19

G. Won 1968 best record Grammy with Art Garfunkel for "Mrs. Robinson" (full name) ....
 ___ ___ ___ ___ ___ ___ ___ ___ ___
 30 4   28 38 36 24 20 31 57

H. Feeble or weak in body or health
 ___ ___ ___ ___ ___ ___
 9   15 49 21 51 41

I. Receive less than the passing grade ....
 ___ ___ ___ ___
 37 8   43 45

Y·E·A·R 1·9·5·4

	1 E	2 H	3 F	4 C	5 H	6 I	7 G	8 B		9 A	10 H	11 D	12 I	13 A
	14 B	15 G	16 H	17 A	18 H	19 E	20 D	21 C	22 F		23 H	24 G		25 F
26 C	27 E	28 I	29 B		30 C	31 A	32 D		33 H	34 B		35 A	36 C	37 G
38 A	39 D		40 E	41 F	42 H	43 A		44 H	45 D	46 G	47 E	48 D	49 B	50 F
	51 E	52 A	53 B		54 H	55 D	56 C	57 I		58 B	59 A	60 D	

A. US vice-president, he killed Alexander Hamilton in an 1804 duel (full name) ....
<u>31</u> <u>38</u> <u>43</u> <u>52</u> <u>17</u> <u>35</u> <u>59</u> <u>9</u> <u>13</u>

B. DeNiro and Redford ....
<u>58</u> <u>34</u> <u>14</u> <u>49</u> <u>53</u> <u>29</u> <u>8</u>

C. Playwright Arthur or big band leader Glenn ....
<u>30</u> <u>26</u> <u>56</u> <u>4</u> <u>21</u> <u>36</u>

D. Forming a fabric by looping a continuous yarn ....
<u>39</u> <u>32</u> <u>45</u> <u>20</u> <u>48</u> <u>55</u> <u>60</u> <u>11</u>

E. Feel pain; undergo a penalty; stand ....
<u>19</u> <u>47</u> <u>51</u> <u>40</u> <u>1</u> <u>27</u>

F. Tailless amphibians having long hind legs adapted for jumping ...
<u>25</u> <u>22</u> <u>41</u> <u>3</u> <u>50</u>

G. Great ____ (large, powerful short-haired dogs) ....
<u>7</u> <u>15</u> <u>46</u> <u>37</u> <u>24</u>

H. "Praise the lord and pass the ____" (said by a navy chaplain at Pearl Harbor) ....
<u>5</u> <u>44</u> <u>54</u> <u>42</u> <u>16</u> <u>23</u> <u>33</u> <u>18</u> <u>10</u>
<u>2</u>

I. "Children should be ___ and not heard" ....
<u>28</u> <u>12</u> <u>57</u> <u>6</u>

51

Y·E·A·R 1·9·7·4

1 J	2 G	3 F	4 A	5 E	6 D	7 G	8 A		9 H	10 G	11 E
	12 K	13 C	14 B	15 D	16 J	17 A	18 G		19 H	20 C	21 B
22 I	23 I	24 H	25 A	26 G	27 B	28 E	29 C		30 H	31 B	32 G
33 I	34 J		35 A	36 C	37 A	38 B		39 A	40 D	41 I	
42 C	43 E	44 G	45 D	46 G	47 K	48 J		49 F	50 A		51 D
52 B	53 E	54 C	55 H	56 G		57 F	58 A	59 D	60 J	61 K	

A. Won best actress Oscars for "Klute" and "Coming Home" (full name) ....
39 58 50 25 35 37 17 8 4

B. One of Bart Simpson's sisters ...
38 21 14 27 31 52

C. Disprove; rebut ....
36 20 42 54 29 13

D. Austrian composer (1756-1791), he wrote over 600 works ....
6 40 45 15 51 59

E. Amusement or laughter; gaiety; rejoicing ....
5 11 43 53 28

F. Objective case of "he" ....
3 49 57

G. British liner sunk by German U-boat (1915), an event that led to US entry into WW1 ....
10 2 18 46 32 7 56 26 44

H. "A soft answer turneth away ___" (Proverbs 1511) ....
24 55 9 30 19

I. Impose a tax ....
33 41 22 23

J. Offense; sin; tort ....
60 48 16 1 34

K. Objective case of "she" ....
61 47 12

52

Y·E·A·R 1·9·7·4

1 G	2 D	3 E	4 H	5 A	■	6 A	7 C	8 H	9 F	10 E	11 E	12 A	■	13 C
14 B	15 F	16 D	■	17 A	18 G	19 D	20 G	21 A	22 A	23 H	24 B	25 E	■	26 A
27 A	28 B	29 A	30 C	31 A	32 E	33 F	34 B	35 E	36 C	■	37 A	38 D	39 E	▬
40 F	41 H	42 A	43 A	44 B	45 A	■	46 C	47 A	48 B	49 E	50 A	51 E	52 A	53 B

A. "The ____ went to sea in a beautiful pea-green boat" (4 wds; from a poem by Edward Lear)

$\overline{27}$ $\overline{17}$ $\overline{21}$ $\overline{31}$ $\overline{52}$ $\overline{45}$ $\overline{37}$ $\overline{50}$ $\overline{22}$

$\overline{26}$ $\overline{29}$ $\overline{12}$ $\overline{42}$ $\overline{5}$ $\overline{6}$ $\overline{47}$ $\overline{43}$

B. 5-digit post office identification (2 wds) ....

$\overline{34}$ $\overline{14}$ $\overline{28}$ $\overline{48}$ $\overline{24}$ $\overline{53}$ $\overline{44}$

C. "Thar she ___!" (lookout's cry when a whale is sighted) ....

$\overline{46}$ $\overline{30}$ $\overline{7}$ $\overline{13}$ $\overline{36}$

D. In the ____ (actively engaged in events) ....

$\overline{16}$ $\overline{38}$ $\overline{2}$ $\overline{19}$

E. 1979 James Bond film, with Roger Moore and "Jaws" ....

$\overline{3}$ $\overline{10}$ $\overline{39}$ $\overline{25}$ $\overline{32}$ $\overline{51}$ $\overline{49}$ $\overline{35}$ $\overline{11}$

F. Mark Twain's Huckleberry ....

$\overline{40}$ $\overline{33}$ $\overline{9}$ $\overline{15}$

G. Triangular sail ....

$\overline{1}$ $\overline{18}$ $\overline{20}$

H. Never ___ (don't bother; it's of no concern) ....

$\overline{4}$ $\overline{41}$ $\overline{8}$ $\overline{23}$

53

Y·E·A·R 1·9·7·6

	1 A	2 B	3 F	4 C	5 A	6 B	7 F	8 C	9 D	10 F		11 G
12 F	13 C	14 B	15 H	16 C	17 A	18 F		19 B	20 G	21 C	22 F	23 G
24 D		25 G	26 H	27 C	28 H	29 G	30 F	31 C		32 B	33 G	34 A
35 E		36 C	37 D	38 F	39 E	40 C	41 A		42 C	43 B		44 C
45 E	46 F	47 B	48 A		49 A	50 D	51 B	52 F	53 A	54 D	55 B	

A. Former name of Zimbabwe .... $\overline{5}$ $\overline{48}$ $\overline{34}$ $\overline{17}$ $\overline{41}$ $\overline{1}$ $\overline{53}$ $\overline{49}$

B. Confuse; darken; make obsure .... $\overline{43}$ $\overline{19}$ $\overline{32}$ $\overline{2}$ $\overline{6}$ $\overline{14}$ $\overline{55}$ $\overline{47}$ $\overline{51}$

C. The Boss .... $\overline{31}$ $\overline{40}$ $\overline{16}$ $\overline{27}$ $\overline{8}$ $\overline{21}$ $\overline{44}$ $\overline{42}$ $\overline{4}$
$\overline{36}$ $\overline{13}$

D. "____ has charms to sooth a
savage breast" (Congreve, "The
Mourning Bride") .... $\overline{50}$ $\overline{37}$ $\overline{24}$ $\overline{9}$ $\overline{54}$

E. What the cow says .... $\overline{35}$ $\overline{39}$ $\overline{45}$

F. San Juan is the capital of this
West Indian commonwealth (2 wds) $\overline{3}$ $\overline{46}$ $\overline{18}$ $\overline{38}$ $\overline{30}$ $\overline{12}$ $\overline{52}$ $\overline{22}$ $\overline{10}$
$\overline{7}$

G. Pertaining to an inhabitant of
Bordeaux, Rouen, or Dijon .... $\overline{25}$ $\overline{33}$ $\overline{20}$ $\overline{23}$ $\overline{11}$ $\overline{29}$

H. Record of the voyage of a
vessel or aircraft .... $\overline{26}$ $\overline{15}$ $\overline{28}$

54

Y·E·A·R 1·9·8·6

	1 I	2 J	3 G	4 C	5 F	6 H	7 C		8 A	9 B	10 B	11 H	12 I
13 E		14 G	15 K	16 C	17 D	18 I	19 K	20 J		21 H	22 G	23 A	24 B
25 E	26 F	27 D	28 K	29 A	30 J	31 H		32 F	33 B	34 C	35 G	36 D	37 A
38 I	39 E	40 C		41 E	42 A	43 J	44 G	45 B	46 J		47 C	48 G	49 F
50 D		51 B	52 A	53 E	54 F		55 D	56 J	57 A	58 E	59 H		

A. The Hoosier State ....
___ ___ ___ ___ ___ ___ ___
23　29　37　57　8　52　42

B. "Candy is dandy but ___ is quicker" (Nash, "Reflections on Ice-Breaking") ....
___ ___ ___ ___ ___ ___
24　51　9　10　45　33

C. Nullify or invalidate; deny the truth of ....
___ ___ ___ ___ ___ ___
7　16　47　4　40　34

D. "Variety's the very ___ of life,/That gives it all its flavor" (Cowper, "The Task") ....
___ ___ ___ ___ ___
50　27　36　17　55

E. English poet (1608-1674), wrote the blank-verse epic "Paradise Lost" ....
___ ___ ___ ___ ___ ___
41　25　58　53　13　39

F. Groucho, Harpo, Chico, and ___ ..
___ ___ ___ ___ ___
5　49　32　26　54

G. Routine work around a house or farm ....
___ ___ ___ ___ ___ ___
44　22　48　3　14　35

H. Composure; dignified, self-confident manner ....
___ ___ ___ ___ ___
21　6　11　31　59

I. Penny ....
___ ___ ___ ___
1　38　12　18

J. Boston's AL team (2 wds) ....
___ ___ ___ ___ ___ ___
43　30　20　46　2　56

K. Norwegian statesman, first UN secretary-general ....
___ ___ ___
15　28　19

Y·E·A·R 1·9·9·1

1 C	2 E	3 F	4 A		5 F	6 A	7 H	8 G	9 C	10 I	11 E	
12 F	13 D	14 I	15 B		16 A	17 A	18 C	19 H		20 F	21 G	22 A
23 H	24 E		25 B	26 D	27 A	28 A	29 B	30 C	31 G		32 A	33 B
34 E	35 A		36 D	37 H	38 A	39 F	40 A	41 I		42 E	43 D	
44 F	45 B	46 H	47 C		48 D	49 I	50 A	51 H	52 B	53 E	54 A	55 C

A. "You are old, ____, the young man said ..." (2 wds; from a poem by Lewis Carroll) ....
___ ___ ___ ___ ___ ___ ___ ___ ___
32 54 50 4 6 17 38 16 28
___ ___ ___ ___
27 40 22 35

B. Sluggishness; inactivity; apathy
___ ___ ___ ___ ___ ___
15 29 52 25 45 33

C. Genial giant lumberjack who worked with his blue ox Babe (US frontier myth) ....
___ ___ ___ ___ ___ ___
1 30 47 55 18 9

D. Burly; big and strong; somewhat hoarse voice ....
___ ___ ___ ___ ___
13 26 48 36 43

E. Hesitates to believe; distrusts; holds questionable ...
___ ___ ___ ___ ___ ___
53 34 2 42 24 11

F. "... and to the republic for which it ___" ....
___ ___ ___ ___ ___ ___
20 12 39 44 5 3

G. Tit for ___ (with an equivalent given in retaliation) ....
___ ___ ___
31 8 21

H. Number of board members required to be present to transact business ....
___ ___ ___ ___ ___ ___
19 37 46 23 51 7

I. Facts, information, statistics, etc. ....
___ ___ ___ ___
10 49 41 14

56

Y·E·A·R 1·9·9·2

	1 H	2 A	3 J	4 I		5 A	6 H	7 K	8 D	9 B	10 E	11 F	12 A
13 H	14 C	15 H	16 D	17 E	18 C	19 J	20 A	21 A	22 B		23 E	24 D		25 G
26 A	27 H	28 K	29 C		30 F	31 A	32 I	33 H	34 J		35 D	36 J	37 B	38 F
39 A	40 A	41 H		42 J	43 A	44 G	45 K	46 C	47 F	48 D		49 A	50 C	51 C
52 G	53 E	54 J	55 B	56 C	57 H	58 G		59 E	60 A	61 B	62 I		63 C	64 D
65 A	66 B	67 I	68 D		69 J	70 A		71 J	72 C	73 F	74 A	75 I	76 H

A. "Be it ever so humble, there's ___" (4 wds; from a song by John Payne) ....

70 2 5 12 20 49 40 39 60

21 31 43 26 65 74

B. Damaged, disfigured ....

37 66 9 55 22 61

C. Veep, in 1992 he spelled "potato" with an "e" on the end (full name) ....

63 50 56 18 46 14 29 51 72

D. Capital city of Iran ....

16 68 48 8 35 64 24

E. Miss a third strike (baseball slang) ....

59 17 23 53 10

F. Warren Beatty starred in this 1991 gangster film ....

38 11 47 73 30

G. "None but the brave deserves the ___" (Dryden, "Alexander's Feast") ....

25 58 52 44

H. Use of actual or threatened violence for political ends .....

76 13 33 27 6 15 57 41 1

I. Have an irritating or unpleasant effect; sound harshly; jar ....

67 75 32 4 62

J. Zealous, painstaking; concerned with learning ....

3 42 36 71 69 54 19 34

K. ___ bits equals twenty-five cents (slang) ....

28 7 45

57

Y·E·A·R   B·I·B·L·I·C·A·L

	1 B	2 H	3 A		4 D	5 F	6 I	7 G		8 A	9 J	10 G	11 E
12 G	13 A	14 C	15 A		16 E	17 B	18 G	19 J	20 C	21 B	22 A	23 E		24 G
25 A		26 F	27 C	28 E	29 A	30 B		31 G	32 I	33 G		34 A	35 G	
36 I	37 B	38 G		39 C	40 E	41 A	42 H	43 C		44 D	45 F	46 B	47 C	
48 A	49 H	50 I	51 A	52 B	53 G		54 C	55 A		56 D	57 I	58 A	59 B	
60 I	61 G	62 A		63 J	64 D	65 A	66 I	67 I	68 A	69 C	70 G			

A. Assembly held to reorganize
Europe after the Napoleonic
Wars (3 wds) ....
‾8‾ ‾55‾ ‾48‾ ‾22‾ ‾41‾ ‾29‾ ‾15‾ ‾13‾ ‾34‾
‾25‾ ‾58‾ ‾51‾ ‾3‾ ‾65‾ ‾62‾ ‾68‾

B. Assign; allot; set apart for a
particular purpose ....
‾21‾ ‾37‾ ‾30‾ ‾52‾ ‾46‾ ‾17‾ ‾1‾ ‾59‾

C. Seat of government of the
Netherlands (2 wds) ....
‾54‾ ‾47‾ ‾14‾ ‾43‾ ‾27‾ ‾69‾ ‾20‾ ‾39‾

D. British hanged him as a spy in
1776 ....
‾56‾ ‾64‾ ‾4‾ ‾44‾

E. "The Fox and the Grapes," for
example ....
‾11‾ ‾40‾ ‾28‾ ‾16‾ ‾23‾

F. A stole or a constrictor ....
‾26‾ ‾5‾ ‾45‾

G. Largest Canadian Atlantic
province ....
‾53‾ ‾70‾ ‾61‾ ‾35‾ ‾24‾ ‾12‾ ‾18‾ ‾7‾ ‾38‾
‾31‾ ‾10‾ ‾33‾

H. Keep it under your ____ ....
‾2‾ ‾49‾ ‾42‾

I. One who sailed with Jason in
search of the Golden Fleece .....
‾57‾ ‾6‾ ‾66‾ ‾60‾ ‾32‾ ‾36‾ ‾67‾ ‾50‾

J. Ship's record ....
‾63‾ ‾9‾ ‾19‾

Y·E·A·R 1·7·7·5

1 C	2 D	3 I	4 B	5 H	6 G	7 E	8 I	9 D		10 H	11 H	12 H
13 G	14 E		15 B	16 G	17 A	18 D	19 C	20 B	21 H		22 A	23 I
	24 G	25 C	26 C	27 G	28 F	29 D	30 B	31 E	32 A		33 C	34 F
35 G		36 B	37 H	38 C	39 A	40 I	41 D	42 G		43 A	44 B	45 H
46 G	47 E	48 A		49 G	50 F	51 H	52 C	53 D		54 G	55 H	56 A
57 D	58 F	59 D	60 B		61 A	62 G	63 G	64 B	65 G	66 A	67 E	

A. Phoenix NFL team; St. Louis NL team ....
 __ __ __ __ __ __ __ __ __
 39 22 61 56 17 32 66 43 48

B. Block or hinder; put obstacles in the way ....
 __ __ __ __ __ __ __ __
 44 15 20 60 64 4 36 30

C. Native of Mazatlán ....
 __ __ __ __ __ __ __
 1 25 26 19 52 33 38

D. Inventing; originating ....
 __ __ __ __ __ __ __ __
 57 41 53 59 18 2 9 29

E. ___ pole (carved and painted post erected by NW North American Indians) ....
 __ __ __ __ __
 14 31 67 47 7

F. "O dark, dark, dark, amid the blaze of ___" (Milton, "Samson Agonistes") ....
 __ __ __ __
 34 58 50 28

G. "... he called for his bowl,/ And he called for his ___" (2 wds; from "Old King Cole") ......
 __ __ __ __ __ __ __ __ __
 49 27 35 42 24 6 16 46 63
 __ __ __ __
 13 54 62 65

H. "He ne'er consider'd it, as loth/To look a ___ in the mouth" (hyph; Samuel Butler, "Hudibras") ....
 __ __ __ __ __ __ __ __ __
 12 11 10 5 21 37 51 45 55

I. Memorandum; annotation; repute; celebrity ....
 __ __ __ __
 3 40 23 8

59

Y·E·A·R 2·0·2·B·C

	1 D	2 F	3 B	4 D	5 B	6 A		7 A	8 B	9 E	10 D	11 H
12 A	13 E	14 F	15 G		16 B	17 B	18 E	19 A	20 F	21 A	22 B	23 D
24 E	25 B	26 G	27 D	28 A	29 F		30 B	31 H		32 C	33 G	34 B
35 D		36 H	37 C	38 G	39 A	40 H	41 D	42 C	43 B	44 D	45 A	46 B
47 A	48 D		49 E	50 H	51 H	52 G	53 A	54 B	55 A	56 D	57 F	

A. She played Mrs. Michael Corleone (full name) ....
 $\overline{55}$ $\overline{45}$ $\overline{12}$ $\overline{19}$ $\overline{53}$ $\overline{28}$ $\overline{21}$ $\overline{7}$ $\overline{39}$
 $\overline{6}$ $\overline{47}$

B. Related subject or problem; consequence; outgrowth ....
 $\overline{22}$ $\overline{46}$ $\overline{34}$ $\overline{5}$ $\overline{8}$ $\overline{43}$ $\overline{16}$ $\overline{30}$ $\overline{25}$
 $\overline{3}$ $\overline{17}$ $\overline{54}$

C. Zig and ___ ....
 $\overline{32}$ $\overline{37}$ $\overline{42}$

D. World's largest inland body of water (2 wds) ....
 $\overline{27}$ $\overline{41}$ $\overline{1}$ $\overline{4}$ $\overline{10}$ $\overline{35}$ $\overline{44}$ $\overline{48}$ $\overline{56}$
 $\overline{23}$

E. Small animals as compared with others of their kind ....
 $\overline{9}$ $\overline{18}$ $\overline{13}$ $\overline{24}$ $\overline{49}$

F. Outer portion of the earth, 22 miles deep under the continents, 6 miles deep under the oceans ....
 $\overline{2}$ $\overline{57}$ $\overline{14}$ $\overline{29}$ $\overline{20}$

G. French city, capital of Pas-de-Calais; wall hanging; marriage gift from husband to wife ....
 $\overline{26}$ $\overline{52}$ $\overline{38}$ $\overline{33}$ $\overline{15}$

H. Staff or support to assist a lame or infirm person in walking
 $\overline{36}$ $\overline{51}$ $\overline{50}$ $\overline{31}$ $\overline{11}$ $\overline{40}$

Y·E·A·R 1·8·6·4

	1 D	2 G	3 B	4 G	5 D	6 F	7 J	8 G	9 D	10 F	11 A	12 E
13 G		14 C	15 H	16 J	17 J	18 F	19 B	20 E	21 A	22 C	23 F		24 H
25 D	26 B	27 A	28 B	29 E	30 C	31 I	32 B		33 F	34 G	35 B	36 F	37 C
38 I	39 B	40 I	41 E		42 A	43 B		44 F	45 C	46 B	47 I	48 F	49 J
50 A	51 I		52 B	53 D		54 A	55 H	56 I	57 J	58 I	59 D		

A. 1985 sci-fi film, rejuvenated
retirees, an Oscar for Don
Ameche ··························· $\overline{27}$ $\overline{42}$ $\overline{54}$ $\overline{11}$ $\overline{50}$ $\overline{21}$

B. "___ With Love" (2 wds; second
James Bond film) ················ $\overline{43}$ $\overline{35}$ $\overline{52}$ $\overline{46}$ $\overline{19}$ $\overline{28}$ $\overline{32}$ $\overline{26}$ $\overline{39}$

$\overline{3}$

C. ___ and Vanzetti (found guilty
in controversial 1921
Massachusetts trial) ············· $\overline{30}$ $\overline{37}$ $\overline{14}$ $\overline{22}$ $\overline{45}$

D. Easily done, performed or used;
skillful in a superficial way ··· $\overline{53}$ $\overline{59}$ $\overline{1}$ $\overline{25}$ $\overline{5}$ $\overline{9}$

E. TV's "Eyewitness ___" ············ $\overline{41}$ $\overline{20}$ $\overline{12}$ $\overline{29}$

F. Instigated rebellion; incited,
provoked, stirred up ············· $\overline{33}$ $\overline{6}$ $\overline{36}$ $\overline{23}$ $\overline{48}$ $\overline{10}$ $\overline{18}$ $\overline{44}$

G. Oliver of the Iran-Contra
scandal ·························· $\overline{13}$ $\overline{34}$ $\overline{4}$ $\overline{8}$ $\overline{2}$

H. "Much ___ About Nothing" (one
of Shakespeare's comedies) ······ $\overline{55}$ $\overline{24}$ $\overline{15}$

I. Spoke in a singing voice;
chanted ·························· $\overline{47}$ $\overline{56}$ $\overline{38}$ $\overline{40}$ $\overline{51}$ $\overline{31}$ $\overline{58}$

J. "___ heart never won fair lady" $\overline{17}$ $\overline{57}$ $\overline{49}$ $\overline{16}$ $\overline{7}$

Y·E·A·R 1·8·8·3

		1 A	2 A	3 B	4 I	5 D	6 A	7 B	8 A		9 A	10 C
11 D		12 A	13 D	14 F		15 A	16 A	17 F	18 G	19 F	20 I	21 H
22 D		23 A	24 G	25 G		26 H	27 D	28 A	29 C	30 I	31 H	32 E
33 F	34 A	35 B	■	36 F	37 C	38 A	39 H		40 D	41 A	42 H	43 F
44 E	45 A	46 E	47 C		48 B	49 D	50 B	51 A	52 B	53 C		

A. Home of the US Air Force Academy (2 wds) ·················
15 2 45 34 41 9 51 16 28
38 1 6 23 8 12

B. Not harmful; kindly; gentle; favorable ·····················
48 3 35 50 52 7

C. "____ wise, pound foolish" ······
29 53 10 47 37

D. _____ Dam was renamed Hoover Dam
40 13 27 5 11 22 49

E. Out of a clear blue ____ (abruptly, without warning) ·····
32 44 46

F. He wrote "Paradise Lost" in 1667
17 33 19 36 43 14

G. Fixed, benchlike seat in a church ·························
18 24 25

H. Cast the first ___ (be the first to blame a wrongdoer) ·····
26 21 42 31 39

I. Have a ___ in one's bonnet (be obsessed with an idea) ··········
4 30 20

Y·E·A·R 1·9·4·9

1 B	2 H	3 E		4 B	5 E	6 A	7 A		8 B	9 A	10 F	11 D
12 A	13 G	14 G	15 B	16 D		17 A	18 H		19 H	20 D	21 C	22 G
23 F		24 D	25 B	26 B		27 A	28 E	29 H		30 A	31 F	32 G
33 H	34 C	35 A	36 H		37 B	38 A	39 F	40 D	41 E	42 C	43 C	
44 A	45 F	46 F	47 E	48 A	49 F	50 C	51 A	52 H	53 F	54 A	55 C	

A. Sean Connery, Roger Moore, George Lazenby, and ___ (full name) ....
<u> </u> <u> </u> <u> </u> <u> </u> <u> </u> <u> </u> <u> </u> <u> </u> <u> </u>
54 17 6 48 27 38 7 30 12

<u> </u> <u> </u> <u> </u> <u> </u>
51 35 9 44

B. Author of the "Canterbury Tales"
<u> </u> <u> </u> <u> </u> <u> </u> <u> </u> <u> </u> <u> </u>
37 25 4 26 8 15 1

C. Tennis star from Vegas, he claims "image is everything" ....
<u> </u> <u> </u> <u> </u> <u> </u> <u> </u> <u> </u>
50 42 34 55 43 21

D. Comes in like a lion and goes out like a lamb ....
<u> </u> <u> </u> <u> </u> <u> </u> <u> </u>
11 40 16 24 20

E. Restaurant built like a railroad car ....
<u> </u> <u> </u> <u> </u> <u> </u> <u> </u>
3 47 41 28 5

F. Evident; apparent; visible ......
<u> </u> <u> </u> <u> </u> <u> </u> <u> </u> <u> </u> <u> </u> <u> </u>
10 45 49 39 23 31 53 46

G. Ward off; provide ....
<u> </u> <u> </u> <u> </u> <u> </u>
32 22 13 14

H. Nickname of General Gordon of Khartoum (1833–1885); residents of Beijing ....
<u> </u> <u> </u> <u> </u> <u> </u> <u> </u> <u> </u> <u> </u>
19 29 52 18 2 36 33

63

Y·E·A·R 1·9·7·3

		1 I	2 E	3 I	4 E	5 C		6 I	7 D	8 A		9 C	10 B
	11 F	12 G	13 C		14 C	15 B	16 A	17 C	18 B	19 C	20 H		21 G
22 D	23 B	24 E	25 H	26 H	27 A	28 D		29 B	30 F		31 C	32 C	33 A
34 D	35 A	36 A	37 C	38 D	39 C	40 G	41 B	42 A	43 A		44 G	■	45 F
46 B	47 I		48 F	49 G	50 C	51 G	52 A	53 G	54 C	55 G	56 E	

A. Caracas is the capital of this
country ....
___ ___ ___ ___ ___ ___ ___ ___ ___
33 43 52 8 42 36 27 35 16

B. Group or clique within a larger
group, party, government, etc. ..
___ ___ ___ ___ ___ ___ ___
10 46 15 29 41 23 18

C. Inscribed basalt slab,
discovered in 1799, key to
Egyptian hieroglyphics (2 wds) ..
___ ___ ___ ___ ___ ___ ___ ___ ___
31 39 14 19 5 13 50 54 37
___ ___ ___
9 17 32

D. Evenings in Paris ....
___ ___ ___ ___ ___
28 34 38 22 7

E. Hit or ___ (haphazardly) ....
___ ___ ___ ___
24 2 56 4

F. Thin rope made of several
strands braided or twisted
together ....
___ ___ ___ ___
11 30 45 48

G. Chinese leader Deng ....
___ ___ ___ ___ ___ ___ ___ ___
44 55 12 53 21 49 40 51

H. Title of a knight ....
___ ___ ___
26 25 20

I. Unrestrained anger or rage;
violence ....
___ ___ ___ ___
1 6 3 47

Y·E·A·R 1·9·9·1

	1 B	2 D	3 B	4 A		5 C	6 H	7 D	8 H	9 A	10 A	11 B
	12 B	13 E		14 D	15 E	16 A		17 H	18 D	19 B	20 E	21 H
	22 F	23 B	24 G	25 C	26 E	27 D		28 F	29 B	30 H		31 C
32 E	33 D	34 B	35 C	36 E		37 A	38 A		39 F	40 G	41 B	42 E
43 F	44 G	45 C		46 A	47 B	48 H	49 F	50 A	51 B	52 E	53 C	

A. Herman Melville's great white whale (2 wds) ....
$\overline{46}\ \overline{16}\ \overline{37}\ \overline{38}\ \overline{4}\ \overline{50}\ \overline{9}\ \overline{10}$

B. Highly distinguished; famous ....
$\overline{47}\ \overline{51}\ \overline{34}\ \overline{19}\ \overline{1}\ \overline{41}\ \overline{29}\ \overline{23}\ \overline{12}$
$\overline{3}\ \overline{11}$

C. Celebration of a saint's day in Mexico ....
$\overline{31}\ \overline{25}\ \overline{35}\ \overline{53}\ \overline{45}\ \overline{5}$

D. Pertaining to a fixed condition; interference due to atmospheric electricity ....
$\overline{27}\ \overline{7}\ \overline{18}\ \overline{14}\ \overline{33}\ \overline{2}$

E. Speculated curiously; pondered; conjectured ....
$\overline{15}\ \overline{32}\ \overline{13}\ \overline{20}\ \overline{26}\ \overline{42}\ \overline{52}\ \overline{36}$

F. Savory jelly made with tomato juice and gelatin, chilled and served as a salad ....
$\overline{28}\ \overline{49}\ \overline{39}\ \overline{43}\ \overline{22}$

G. Cereal grass cultivated for its edible seed ....
$\overline{44}\ \overline{40}\ \overline{24}$

H. Afternoon nap in Mexico ....
$\overline{17}\ \overline{21}\ \overline{30}\ \overline{48}\ \overline{6}\ \overline{8}$

65

Y·E·A·R B·I·B·L·I·C·A·L

	1 E	2 C	3 A	4 B	5 G		6 C	7 I	8 F	9 E	10 G
11 C	12 I	13 A	14 F	15 B	16 D	17 J	18 B	19 J		20 E	21 D
22 I	23 A	24 B	25 F	26 D		27 H	28 F	29 G		30 A	31 D
32 H	33 I	34 F	35 B	36 C	37 D	38 A	39 I	40 C		41 B	42 A
43 F	44 J	45 B	46 G	47 H		48 F	49 A	50 E	51 J	52 F	

A. Mount ____ (highest mountain in the US outside Alaska) ··········
  38 49 30 23 3 13 42

B. Assail persistently; explain, worry about, or work at something repeatedly ············
  15 45 35 4 41 24 18

C. Noah saw it coming ··············
  6 36 11 2 40

D. Mars has two of these ···········
  26 16 37 21 31

E. Monopoly card: "... Go directly to ___. Do not pass Go" ·········
  1 50 20 9

F. One who argues or disputes; a US cowboy ·······················
  48 25 34 28 43 8 52 14

G. Short race, as 100 yards ········
  29 46 10 5

H. ETS roadblock to high school seniors ························
  32 27 47

I. "Rule, Britannia, rule the ____; Britons never will be slaves." ·····················
  33 7 12 39 22

J. Rendered fat of hogs ············
  51 17 44 19

Y·E·A·R 1·7·7·3

1 F	2 C	3 D	4 B	5 A	6 G	7 D	8 C	9 H		10 E	11 A	12 G
13 H	14 E		15 F	16 D	17 F	18 E	19 A	20 I	21 H		22 A	23 A	24 A
25 A	26 F		27 E	28 B	29 I		30 D	31 D	32 A	33 G		34 A	35 A
36 H		37 D	38 A	39 E	40 G	41 B		42 I	43 G	44 A	45 G		46 B
47 E	48 C	49 G	50 A	51 G		52 I	53 D	54 F	55 H	56 C	57 A	

A. "I come to bury Caesar, _____ "
(4 wds; "Julius Caesar" III ii) .

$\overline{5}$ $\overline{50}$ $\overline{44}$ $\overline{34}$ $\overline{11}$ $\overline{25}$ $\overline{57}$ $\overline{38}$ $\overline{19}$

$\overline{22}$ $\overline{35}$ $\overline{23}$ $\overline{24}$ $\overline{32}$

B. Lead singer of U2 ....

$\overline{46}$ $\overline{4}$ $\overline{28}$ $\overline{41}$

C. Capital city of Norway ....

$\overline{2}$ $\overline{48}$ $\overline{8}$ $\overline{56}$

D. Classic Bram Stoker novel; Bela
Lugosi starred as a vampire in
the film ....

$\overline{30}$ $\overline{16}$ $\overline{7}$ $\overline{37}$ $\overline{31}$ $\overline{3}$ $\overline{53}$

E. Brigitte ___ (sexy 50s French
film actress) ....

$\overline{10}$ $\overline{27}$ $\overline{39}$ $\overline{14}$ $\overline{47}$ $\overline{18}$

F. Children's beds with enclosed
sides; bins for storing grain ...

$\overline{1}$ $\overline{54}$ $\overline{17}$ $\overline{15}$ $\overline{26}$

G. Extremely moving; affecting the
emotions; sharp or piquant ......

$\overline{33}$ $\overline{45}$ $\overline{6}$ $\overline{40}$ $\overline{51}$ $\overline{12}$ $\overline{43}$ $\overline{49}$

H. Impetuous; rash; impudent;
tactless ....

$\overline{55}$ $\overline{13}$ $\overline{36}$ $\overline{9}$ $\overline{21}$

I. Type of antenna used in
transmitting or receiving TV,
radio, or microwave signals .....

$\overline{29}$ $\overline{42}$ $\overline{20}$ $\overline{52}$

67

Y·E·A·R 1·8·6·3

	1 A	2 E	3 C	4 B	5 F	6 D	7 G	8 H	9 G		10 B	11 C
12 A	13 D	14 G	15 F	16 A		17 F	18 F	19 H	20 A		21 B	22 F
	23 C	24 H	25 F	26 F	27 A	28 E	29 F	30 A	31 B	32 D		33 F
34 A	35 E	36 C	37 C	38 F		39 B	40 A		41 D	42 G	43 A	44 E
45 F	46 B	47 G	48 C	49 A	50 D	51 H	52 C	53 F	54 B	55 A	56 C	

A. Legal proceeding filed on behalf on many (2 wds) ....
 __ __ __ __ __ __ __ __ __
 12 55 43 1 20 34 27 40 30
 __ __
 49 16

B. Light spear thrown by hand (an Olympic field event) ....
 __ __ __ __ __ __ __
 10 39 31 46 54 21 4

C. Quick to evaporate; highly unstable; explosive; mercurial ..
 __ __ __ __ __ __ __ __
 52 3 37 11 36 23 48 56

D. "I'm a rambling ____ from Georgia Tech" ....
 __ __ __ __ __
 6 50 32 41 13

E. A color diluted with white; hue .
 __ __ __ __
 35 28 44 2

F. Civil _____ (Gandhi's political tool) ....
 __ __ __ __ __ __ __ __ __
 17 53 29 15 33 38 25 18 5
 __ __ __
 22 45 26

G. ___ of ivy (college or university) ....
 __ __ __ __ __
 42 7 47 9 14

H. Crystalline body that focuses light rays in the eye ....
 __ __ __ __
 8 19 24 51

68

Y·E·A·R 1·9·5·1

	1 A	2 J	3 C	4 H	5 A	6 A	▄	7 E	8 F	9 D	10 J	11 E	12 A
13 A	14 C	15 I	16 H	17 G	18 E	19 F	20 C	21 B		22 A	23 E		24 D	25 E
26 A	27 C	28 G	29 A	30 E	31 F		32 A	33 D		34 B	35 H	36 E	37 A	38 D
39 C		40 B	41 A	42 A	43 J	44 E		45 J	46 I		47 B	48 E	49 G	50 F
51 E	52 A	53 I		54 D	55 J	56 C	57 A	58 E	59 F	60 B	61 I	62 A		63 H
64 H	65 B	66 J		67 E	68 A	69 A	70 G		71 C	72 A	73 F	74 H	75 D

A. Walter Cronkite's 6-word closing

42 32 12 26 68 69 5 57 1

41 52 72 13 6 22 62 29

37

B. Jennings, O'Toole, and Rabbit ...

34 47 21 60 65 40

C. Well-known and respected; distinguished; outstanding ......

56 14 27 20 3 39 71

D. Locomotive inventor Peter or '30s-'50s movie star Gary ....

9 33 38 54 75 24

E. "The Lay of the ____" (2 wds; metrical romance by Sir Walter Scott) ....

44 25 7 51 18 58 11 23 67

36 30 48

F. Determine or settle; conclude; resolve ....

59 8 50 73 31 19

G. Ward off; resist ....

28 49 70 17

H. Swindlers (slang, 2 wds) ....

74 64 16 63 35 4

I. A friend in ___ is a friend indeed ....

61 15 46 53

J. Derby (head-warmer in London) ..

45 10 2 43 66 55

Y·E·A·R 1·9·6·2

1 D	2 A	3 E	4 G	5 F	6 C		7 C	8 D	9 E	10 B	11 I
12 A	13 C	14 E	15 G	16 D	17 H	18 F	19 B	20 D	21 G	22 E	23 C
24 H	25 D		26 D	27 E	28 B	29 F	30 D	31 H	32 B		33 H	34 D
35 E		36 H	37 F	38 D	39 B	40 A		41 G	42 I		43 F	44 B
45 G	46 F	47 D		48 A	49 B	50 H	51 A	52 D	53 H	54 I	55 I	56 C

A. His abduction of Helen led to
the Trojan War .... ___ ___ ___ ___ ___
48 40 2 12 51

B. "Oh my ____ Clementine" .... ___ ___ ___ ___ ___ ___ ___
19 32 49 39 44 10 28

C. Treaty of __ (formally ended
the War of 1812) .... ___ ___ ___ ___ ___
7 6 23 13 56

D. Spread or grow rapidly .... ___ ___ ___ ___ ___ ___ ___ ___ ___
16 30 25 38 52 1 20 8 26

___ ___
47 34

E. "My ___ burns at both ends;/It
will not last the night"
(Millay) .... ___ ___ ___ ___ ___ ___
22 9 35 14 27 3

F. "Good ___ make good neighbours"
(Frost, "Mending Wall") .... ___ ___ ___ ___ ___ ___
43 29 18 5 37 46

G. Situated farther within;
hidden; private .... ___ ___ ___ ___ ___
41 4 21 15 45

H. When the water returns to the
sea (2 wds) .... ___ ___ ___ ___ ___ ___ ___
17 36 33 24 31 53 50

I. Dispatched; transmitted .... ___ ___ ___ ___
42 54 55 11

Y·E·A·R 1·9·8·0

1 B	2 C	3 A	4 H	5 F	6 D	7 E	8 F		9 F	10 A		11 C	12 A	13 A
14 G	15 F	16 B	17 E		18 D	19 H	20 F	21 E	22 B	23 A	24 H		25 H	26 A
27 E	28 B	29 G		30 C	31 A	32 G	33 B	34 D		35 F	36 D	37 A	38 F	39 F
40 H	41 B	42 D		43 F	44 A		45 C	46 G	47 D		48 B	49 F	50 E	51 D

A. NCAA basketball semifinalists
(2 wds) .... $\overline{10}$ $\overline{13}$ $\overline{3}$ $\overline{26}$ $\overline{23}$ $\overline{37}$ $\overline{44}$ $\overline{31}$ $\overline{12}$

B. Everybody talks about it, but
nobody does anything about it ... $\overline{48}$ $\overline{41}$ $\overline{33}$ $\overline{16}$ $\overline{1}$ $\overline{22}$ $\overline{28}$

C. Fairy in Shakespeare's "A
Midsummer Night's Dream" .... $\overline{11}$ $\overline{2}$ $\overline{30}$ $\overline{45}$

D. Threescore and ten .... $\overline{42}$ $\overline{6}$ $\overline{18}$ $\overline{36}$ $\overline{34}$ $\overline{51}$ $\overline{47}$

E. Put on formal clothes; adorn .... $\overline{7}$ $\overline{27}$ $\overline{17}$ $\overline{50}$ $\overline{21}$

F. Substitutes; deputies; those
appointed to act for others ..... $\overline{8}$ $\overline{38}$ $\overline{5}$ $\overline{35}$ $\overline{9}$ $\overline{39}$ $\overline{15}$ $\overline{43}$ $\overline{49}$
$\overline{20}$

G. Flock of birds; group of girls .. $\overline{32}$ $\overline{46}$ $\overline{14}$ $\overline{29}$

H. Yields or formally surrenders
to another .... $\overline{25}$ $\overline{40}$ $\overline{4}$ $\overline{19}$ $\overline{24}$

Y·E·A·R B·I·B·L·I·C·A·L

		1 E	2 I	3 D	4 F	5 H	6 D	7 B		8 J	9 D	10 C	11 B
12 B	13 F	14 C	15 G	16 D	17 K	18 B		19 E	20 D	21 C	22 A	23 B	24 D
25 F	26 G	27 K	28 D		29 H	30 B	31 I	32 G	33 F		34 D	35 H	36 J
37 A		38 I	39 B	40 D		41 J	42 K	43 H	44 I	45 C		46 A	47 J
48 G	49 I	50 K	51 G		52 A	53 D		54 F	55 B	56 G	57 G		58 H
59 F	60 B	61 E	62 A	63 K	64 C		65 D	66 B	67 E	68 C	69 A		

A. "Every Rose Has Its Thorn" was
their 1989 hit single .... $\overline{69}$ $\overline{52}$ $\overline{22}$ $\overline{37}$ $\overline{62}$ $\overline{46}$

B. Make or declare sacred;
venerate; sanctify .... $\overline{23}$ $\overline{30}$ $\overline{39}$ $\overline{18}$ $\overline{11}$ $\overline{12}$ $\overline{7}$ $\overline{55}$ $\overline{60}$

$\overline{66}$

C. Reliable .... $\overline{64}$ $\overline{10}$ $\overline{68}$ $\overline{14}$ $\overline{21}$ $\overline{45}$

D. He wrote "Robinson Crusoe" in
1719 and "Moll Flanders" in
1722 (full name) .... $\overline{34}$ $\overline{3}$ $\overline{20}$ $\overline{24}$ $\overline{28}$ $\overline{65}$ $\overline{40}$ $\overline{16}$ $\overline{53}$

$\overline{9}$ $\overline{6}$

E. Melt; become less hostile or
tense .... $\overline{67}$ $\overline{61}$ $\overline{19}$ $\overline{1}$

F. Equality, as in amount, status
or character; equivalence .... $\overline{25}$ $\overline{13}$ $\overline{54}$ $\overline{59}$ $\overline{4}$ $\overline{33}$

G. Trying or testing the flavor or
quality of something by taking
some into the mouth .... $\overline{15}$ $\overline{26}$ $\overline{51}$ $\overline{32}$ $\overline{56}$ $\overline{57}$ $\overline{48}$

H. San Francisco's Fisherman's
_____ .... $\overline{58}$ $\overline{5}$ $\overline{35}$ $\overline{43}$ $\overline{29}$

I. Bret ___ (American author; "The
Luck of Roaring Camp"; 1868) .... $\overline{49}$ $\overline{38}$ $\overline{31}$ $\overline{44}$ $\overline{2}$

J. Full of unresolved questions;
doubtful (informal) .... $\overline{47}$ $\overline{8}$ $\overline{41}$ $\overline{36}$

K. Brown, cutthroat, brook, or
rainbow .... $\overline{27}$ $\overline{17}$ $\overline{42}$ $\overline{63}$ $\overline{50}$

Y·E·A·R B·I·B·L·I·C·A·L

	1 B	2 C	3 A	4 C	5 G	6 D	7 A	■	8 I	9 E	10 G	11 B	12 F
13 G	14 H	15 D	16 I	17 A	18 A	■	19 D	20 C	21 G	22 B	23 A	24 C	25 H	26 H
27 G	■	28 F	29 B	■	30 E	31 D	32 G	33 A	34 E	■	35 C	36 D	37 G	38 A
■	39 A	40 B	41 H	42 G	43 I	■	44 A	45 C	46 E	■	47 D	48 A	49 C	
50 H	51 E	52 B	53 D	■	54 G	55 F	56 A	■	57 H	58 D	59 G	60 A	

A. He played "Bugsy" (full name) ...
$\overline{33}\ \overline{44}\ \overline{56}\ \overline{3}\ \overline{23}\ \overline{38}\ \overline{39}\ \overline{60}\ \overline{48}$
$\overline{17}\ \overline{7}\ \overline{18}$

B. "The Rolling ___" ....
$\overline{52}\ \overline{22}\ \overline{29}\ \overline{11}\ \overline{40}\ \overline{1}$

C. Ancient Roman god of the sea ....
$\overline{24}\ \overline{20}\ \overline{4}\ \overline{49}\ \overline{35}\ \overline{45}\ \overline{2}$

D. Unspoiled; having its original
purity ....
$\overline{36}\ \overline{31}\ \overline{15}\ \overline{19}\ \overline{53}\ \overline{58}\ \overline{6}\ \overline{47}$

E. "I wandered lonely as a
___/That floats on high o'er
vales and hills (Wordsworth) ....
$\overline{30}\ \overline{34}\ \overline{9}\ \overline{51}\ \overline{46}$

F. Speck; small roundish mark made
with a pen ....
$\overline{12}\ \overline{55}\ \overline{28}$

G. Body of water between Yemen and
Somalia at entrance to the Red
Sea (3 wds) ....
$\overline{13}\ \overline{10}\ \overline{42}\ \overline{59}\ \overline{37}\ \overline{54}\ \overline{32}\ \overline{27}\ \overline{5}$
$\overline{21}$

H. Picked; gathered the choice
things from ....
$\overline{25}\ \overline{14}\ \overline{41}\ \overline{57}\ \overline{26}\ \overline{50}$

I. "'Will you walk into my
parlour?' said a spider to a
___" (from a poem by Mary
Howitt) ....
$\overline{8}\ \overline{16}\ \overline{43}$

Y·E·A·R 1·9·4·0

1 A	2 C	3 G	4 G		5 G	6 B	7 A	8 F	9 E		10 H	11 A
	12 F	13 G	14 B	15 E	16 C	17 C	18 F		19 A	20 D	21 H	22 G
23 C	24 D	25 D	26 H	27 A		28 D	29 B	30 F		31 C	32 G	33 B
34 E		35 F	36 A	37 C	38 E		39 C	40 C	41 B	42 G	43 D	

A. Gifford and Sinatra .... $\overline{11}$ $\overline{7}$ $\overline{19}$ $\overline{36}$ $\overline{1}$ $\overline{27}$

B. "Remember the ____!"
(Spanish-American War cry) ...... $\overline{14}$ $\overline{6}$ $\overline{41}$ $\overline{29}$ $\overline{33}$

C. Thrilling; stirring .... $\overline{39}$ $\overline{40}$ $\overline{23}$ $\overline{2}$ $\overline{37}$ $\overline{17}$ $\overline{16}$ $\overline{31}$

D. Subside; reduce; diminish .... $\overline{28}$ $\overline{20}$ $\overline{24}$ $\overline{25}$ $\overline{43}$

E. Landlocked SE Asia country
whose capital is Vientiane ...... $\overline{9}$ $\overline{15}$ $\overline{38}$ $\overline{34}$

F. Amos and Andy, Fibber McGee,
Jack Benny, and Fred Allen were
stars of this medium .... $\overline{12}$ $\overline{18}$ $\overline{30}$ $\overline{35}$ $\overline{8}$

G. ____ one's heels (being kept
waiting) .... $\overline{5}$ $\overline{13}$ $\overline{32}$ $\overline{42}$ $\overline{22}$ $\overline{3}$ $\overline{4}$

H. Wordsworth's "___: Intimations
of Immortality" .... $\overline{10}$ $\overline{21}$ $\overline{26}$

Y·E·A·R 1·8·6·5

1 F	2 A	3 E	4 D	5 H	6 I	7 B	8 A	9 H		10 G	11 C	12 B	13 A
14 A	15 E	16 H		17 H	18 G		19 C	20 B	21 I	22 H		23 E	24 B
25 G		26 C	27 E	28 A	29 B	30 D	31 I		32 G	33 B		34 H	35 H
36 H	37 C	38 E		39 D	40 B	41 A	42 F	43 H	44 D	45 A		46 B	47 C
48 D	49 B	50 E	51 F	52 A	53 G		54 C	55 D	56 A	57 B	58 H	59 D	60 F

A. Settle a quarrel; end hostility . $\overline{2}\ \overline{45}\ \overline{56}\ \overline{14}\ \overline{8}\ \overline{13}\ \overline{52}\ \overline{28}\ \overline{41}$

B. "I regret that I have but one life to lose for my country" (full name; last words in 1776) . $\overline{24}\ \overline{46}\ \overline{33}\ \overline{40}\ \overline{57}\ \overline{12}\ \overline{20}\ \overline{49}\ \overline{29}$ $\overline{7}$

C. He was skilled in flattery because he ____ the Blarney Stone .... $\overline{26}\ \overline{11}\ \overline{19}\ \overline{47}\ \overline{54}\ \overline{37}$

D. Long locks or curls of unbound hair .... $\overline{39}\ \overline{44}\ \overline{30}\ \overline{48}\ \overline{55}\ \overline{59}\ \overline{4}$

E. Collie hero of films and a TV series .... $\overline{15}\ \overline{23}\ \overline{50}\ \overline{38}\ \overline{27}\ \overline{3}$

F. To forego one's opportunity to bid in bridge .... $\overline{1}\ \overline{42}\ \overline{60}\ \overline{51}$

G. ____ End (the SW tip of England) $\overline{10}\ \overline{32}\ \overline{53}\ \overline{25}\ \overline{18}$

H. "All the news that's ____" (3 wds; motto of "The New York Times") .... $\overline{34}\ \overline{17}\ \overline{22}\ \overline{43}\ \overline{35}\ \overline{58}\ \overline{36}\ \overline{5}\ \overline{16}$ $\overline{9}$

I. A number that leaves a remainder of 1 when divided by 2 $\overline{21}\ \overline{6}\ \overline{31}$

75

Y·E·A·R 1·9·6·5

	1 G	2 C	3 D	4 F		5 B	6 G	7 F	8 C	9 B	10 D	11 E	12 A
	13 J	14 G	15 B	16 E		17 D	18 F	19 B		20 D	21 A	22 C	23 D
24 B	25 E	26 J		27 B	28 A	29 G	30 H		31 B	32 D	33 G	34 A	35 E
36 I	37 E	38 I	39 D	40 A	41 B	42 I		43 G	44 A		45 J	46 H	47 I
48 F	49 D	50 C	51 I		52 B	53 B	54 D	55 H	56 I	57 D	58 G	

A. Jefferson or the Supreme Court's Clarence ....
— — — — — —
44 40 28 34 21 12

B. State of carelessness, avoiding duty or responsibility ....
— — — — — — — — —
15 19 27 9 41 52 24 5 31
—
53

C. Take to ____ (blame; censure) ...
— — — —
50 2 22 8

D. "An army marches on ____" (2 wds; attributed to Napoleon) ....
— — — — — — — — —
57 17 49 39 23 54 20 10 3
—
32

E. "It never rains, but it ___" ....
— — — — —
35 37 11 25 16

F. ____ Finn (Tom Sawyer's best friend) ....
— — — —
18 48 7 4

G. Basque game played with a long, curved wicker basket (2 wds) ....
— — — — — — —
1 33 6 58 29 43 14

H. Make the ___ fly (cause a violent scene; make trouble) ....
— — —
30 46 55

I. Summoning by repeatedly calling out the person's name ....
— — — — — —
42 51 56 36 38 47

J. Maxim; proverb ....
— — —
26 45 13

76

Y·E·A·R 1·9·7·3

1 H	2 I	3 B	4 A	5 I	6 D	7 F	8 E		9 C	10 H	11 B	12 D
13 C		14 H	15 H	16 A	17 E	18 D	19 E	20 B		21 G	22 A	23 D
24 A		25 H	26 I		27 E	28 B	29 H	30 H	31 D	32 A		33 D
34 G	35 E	36 E	37 D	38 F	39 G	40 F		41 C	42 E	43 D	44 F	45 B
	46 C	47 I		48 G	49 A	50 C	51 D	52 G	53 F	54 B	55 D

A. It replaced Istanbul as its nation's capital in 1923 ....
49 32 24 4 16 22

B. The Dog Star, brightest star in the heavens ....
20 28 3 11 54 45

C. Device that makes possible the transmission of computer data via telephone ....
41 46 9 13 50

D. Wavers; is indecisive; hesitates
12 51 23 31 43 6 18 37 33
55

E. Desiring; craving ....
27 17 8 36 42 19 35

F. Your sister's daughter ....
40 7 44 53 38

G. ____ one's time (waits for a favorable opportunity) ....
21 34 48 39 52

H. Craving liquid; parched; eagerly desirous ....
29 30 1 10 14 25 15

I. Enemies; adversaries; opponents .
47 26 5 2

77

Y·E·A·R 1·7·9·3

	1 A	2 D	3 B	4 G	5 G		6 B	7 H		8 G	9 B	10 C	11 A	12 E
13 H	14 D		15 F	16 A		17 H	18 E	19 F	20 B	21 C		22 A	23 B	
24 D	25 B	26 F		27 G	28 E	29 D	30 F		31 H	32 F		33 C	34 E	35 B
36 D	37 A	38 A	39 B	40 E	41 G		42 A	43 B	44 C	45 E	46 A	47 C		

A. Its capital city is Bogota ......
   $\overline{42}\ \overline{16}\ \overline{37}\ \overline{38}\ \overline{1}\ \overline{11}\ \overline{22}\ \overline{46}$

B. Gradual wearing away; decrease
   in numbers or size ....
   $\overline{35}\ \overline{39}\ \overline{9}\ \overline{3}\ \overline{25}\ \overline{20}\ \overline{6}\ \overline{43}\ \overline{23}$

C. Careful; wary; cautious ....
   $\overline{33}\ \overline{21}\ \overline{10}\ \overline{44}\ \overline{47}$

D. Vader of "Star Wars" ....
   $\overline{14}\ \overline{2}\ \overline{36}\ \overline{29}\ \overline{24}$

E. Immersed the body in water;
   washed ....
   $\overline{12}\ \overline{28}\ \overline{40}\ \overline{34}\ \overline{18}\ \overline{45}$

F. Quick; hurried; precipitate .....
   $\overline{30}\ \overline{19}\ \overline{26}\ \overline{15}\ \overline{32}$

G. Encourages or supports by aid
   or approval, usually in
   wrongdoing; helps ....
   $\overline{4}\ \overline{27}\ \overline{41}\ \overline{5}\ \overline{8}$

H. Resting places; layers of rock;
   pieces of ground in which
   plants are grown ....
   $\overline{31}\ \overline{13}\ \overline{17}\ \overline{7}$

Y·E·A·R 1·8·2·0

1 D	2 F	3 A	4 B	5 C		6 F	7 I	8 B	9 D	10 G	11 E	12 H
13 I	14 H		15 A	16 I	17 B	18 C	19 D		20 E	21 H	22 B	23 A
24 E	25 I	26 B	27 H	28 E	29 H		30 B	31 C	32 B	33 E	34 F	
35 A	36 H	37 C	38 F	39 H	40 B		41 H	42 H	43 G		44 F	45 H
46 G	47 F	48 B	49 H	50 F		51 A	52 B	53 I	54 C	55 E	56 D	57 B

A. Fighting ___ of Notre Dame ......
$\overline{23}\ \overline{35}\ \overline{3}\ \overline{51}\ \overline{15}$

B. Not genuine; forged ....
$\overline{32}\ \overline{26}\ \overline{52}\ \overline{17}\ \overline{40}\ \overline{8}\ \overline{22}\ \overline{30}\ \overline{57}$
$\overline{48}\ \overline{4}$

C. Oliver Goldsmith's "The ___ of
Wakefield" (1766) ....
$\overline{37}\ \overline{5}\ \overline{54}\ \overline{31}\ \overline{18}$

D. "Don't ___ the dirt with the
rest of those girls" (from Cole
Porter's "The Lady Is a Tramp") .
$\overline{56}\ \overline{19}\ \overline{9}\ \overline{1}$

E. Scolds; finds fault; rebukes ....
$\overline{20}\ \overline{28}\ \overline{55}\ \overline{11}\ \overline{33}\ \overline{24}$

F. It points to magnetic north .....
$\overline{44}\ \overline{38}\ \overline{47}\ \overline{6}\ \overline{2}\ \overline{34}\ \overline{50}$

G. Take a ___ view of (regard with
pessimism or skepticism) ....
$\overline{43}\ \overline{10}\ \overline{46}$

H. "Where the deer and _____ play"
(2 wds) ....
$\overline{14}\ \overline{21}\ \overline{36}\ \overline{41}\ \overline{42}\ \overline{49}\ \overline{29}\ \overline{39}\ \overline{45}$
$\overline{27}\ \overline{12}$

I. Inactive; immobile; not
reacting chemically ....
$\overline{53}\ \overline{13}\ \overline{16}\ \overline{7}\ \overline{25}$

Y·E·A·R 1·8·3·6

		1 G	2 F	3 B	4 E		5 D	6 A	7 H	8 C	9 J	10 B	11 H	12 J
	13 J	14 B	15 E		16 H	17 C	18 F		19 I	20 G	21 B	22 H	23 A	
24 C	25 E	26 B	27 A	28 A		29 C	30 H	31 D	32 G	33 F	34 H		35 A	36 B
37 D	38 D	39 A		40 B	41 E	42 D		43 C	44 J		45 E	46 D	47 C	48 A
49 J	50 I	51 H	52 A		53 B	54 H		55 C	56 B	57 I	58 B	59 F	

A. Detroit's NHL team (2 wds) ......
$\overline{6}$ $\overline{23}$ $\overline{39}$ $\overline{35}$ $\overline{48}$ $\overline{27}$ $\overline{28}$ $\overline{52}$

B. "... without the help and support of the ____" (3 wds; from Edward VIII's farewell broadcast) ....
$\overline{21}$ $\overline{40}$ $\overline{58}$ $\overline{53}$ $\overline{14}$ $\overline{36}$ $\overline{56}$ $\overline{26}$ $\overline{3}$
$\overline{10}$

C. Public passenger automobile, usually fitted with a meter .....
$\overline{29}$ $\overline{24}$ $\overline{47}$ $\overline{17}$ $\overline{8}$ $\overline{55}$ $\overline{43}$

D. Exclude; leave out ....
$\overline{46}$ $\overline{31}$ $\overline{5}$ $\overline{38}$ $\overline{37}$ $\overline{42}$

E. Ventriloquist's partner ....
$\overline{15}$ $\overline{41}$ $\overline{45}$ $\overline{25}$ $\overline{4}$

F. Low, inarticulate sound of suffering ....
$\overline{18}$ $\overline{59}$ $\overline{2}$ $\overline{33}$

G. Busy activity; bustle; fuss .....
$\overline{32}$ $\overline{1}$ $\overline{20}$

H. Throw off an obstacle or burden .
$\overline{16}$ $\overline{30}$ $\overline{11}$ $\overline{54}$ $\overline{22}$ $\overline{34}$ $\overline{7}$ $\overline{51}$

I. Bleating cry of a sheep ....
$\overline{19}$ $\overline{57}$ $\overline{50}$

J. Adhesive; sticky; not tasteful or fashionable ....
$\overline{12}$ $\overline{13}$ $\overline{49}$ $\overline{9}$ $\overline{44}$

Y·E·A·R 1·8·7·6

		1 D	2 F	3 I	4 G	5 H	6 C			7 A	8 F	9 B			10 H
11 H	12 C	13 F	14 B	15 A		16 I	17 D	18 B	19 J	20 G			21 C	22 A
23 H	24 B	25 A		26 J	27 D	28 B		29 H	30 F		31 H	32 H	33 B
34 E	35 A		36 I	37 B	38 E	39 C	40 D		41 J	42 H	43 A	44 B	45 E
	46 C	47 B	48 A	49 I	50 H		51 A	52 E		53 H	54 C	55 D	56 G
57 A	58 H		59 F	60 B	61 F		62 H	63 J	64 H	65 A			

A. This city's lighthouse was one of the Seven Wonders of the World ....
$\overline{7}$ $\overline{57}$ $\overline{15}$ $\overline{35}$ $\overline{43}$ $\overline{65}$ $\overline{25}$ $\overline{48}$ $\overline{22}$
$\overline{51}$

B. The part of the earth's surface between the tropics of Cancer and Capricorn (2 wds) ....
$\overline{28}$ $\overline{33}$ $\overline{14}$ $\overline{18}$ $\overline{60}$ $\overline{9}$ $\overline{44}$ $\overline{47}$ $\overline{37}$
$\overline{24}$

C. "Age cannot ___ her, nor custom stale/ Her infinite variety" (Antony and Cleopatra" II, ii) ..
$\overline{21}$ $\overline{54}$ $\overline{12}$ $\overline{46}$ $\overline{39}$ $\overline{6}$

D. Seek the affections of; woo .....
$\overline{1}$ $\overline{17}$ $\overline{27}$ $\overline{40}$ $\overline{55}$

E. Task which one is expected to perform ....
$\overline{38}$ $\overline{34}$ $\overline{52}$ $\overline{45}$

F. ____ power (ability to purchase goods and services) ....
$\overline{59}$ $\overline{2}$ $\overline{30}$ $\overline{13}$ $\overline{8}$ $\overline{61}$

G. ___ offensive (Vietnam, January 30, 1968) ....
$\overline{4}$ $\overline{20}$ $\overline{56}$

H. Deserving of blame, rebuke, or censure; culpable ....
$\overline{42}$ $\overline{50}$ $\overline{23}$ $\overline{64}$ $\overline{58}$ $\overline{62}$ $\overline{5}$ $\overline{11}$ $\overline{31}$
$\overline{32}$ $\overline{29}$ $\overline{53}$ $\overline{10}$

I. "No muss, no ___" ....
$\overline{16}$ $\overline{36}$ $\overline{3}$ $\overline{49}$

J. French fashion designer Chanel ..
$\overline{19}$ $\overline{63}$ $\overline{41}$ $\overline{26}$

81

Y·E·A·R 1·8·9·2

	1 G	2 C	3 J	4 I	5 K	6 H	7 C		8 G	9 A	10 D	11 I	12 I	13 G
	14 E	15 I	16 C		17 G	18 E	19 D	20 C	21 G	22 A	23 G	24 G		25 K
26 J		27 B	28 A	29 G	30 H	31 C	32 C		33 J	34 B	35 C	36 E	37 A	
38 C	39 I	40 A	41 D	42 J	43 C	44 B	45 A	46 F	47 C	48 J		49 G	50 C	51 A
52 F		53 B	54 E	55 E	56 G	57 D		58 E	59 C	60 K		61 B	62 E	63 I
64 D	65 G	66 C	67 B	68 F	69 G	70 C	71 I		72 H	73 D	74 B	75 A	76 C

A. Gondolier; ornamental glassware
   from the island of Murano ....
   $\overline{22}$ $\overline{75}$ $\overline{51}$ $\overline{28}$ $\overline{37}$ $\overline{45}$ $\overline{40}$ $\overline{9}$

B. Argue over something unimportant
   $\overline{61}$ $\overline{53}$ $\overline{34}$ $\overline{27}$ $\overline{67}$ $\overline{74}$ $\overline{44}$

C. Popular name for famous 1872
   portrait "Arrangement in Gray
   and Black" (2 wds) ....
   $\overline{43}$ $\overline{38}$ $\overline{50}$ $\overline{66}$ $\overline{7}$ $\overline{20}$ $\overline{32}$ $\overline{70}$ $\overline{76}$
   $\overline{31}$ $\overline{2}$ $\overline{16}$ $\overline{47}$ $\overline{59}$ $\overline{35}$

D. Historic European museum, home
   of the Venus de Milo and Mona
   Lisa ....
   $\overline{19}$ $\overline{10}$ $\overline{73}$ $\overline{41}$ $\overline{57}$ $\overline{64}$

E. Infirm; defective; fallacious;
   unreliable ....
   $\overline{18}$ $\overline{54}$ $\overline{36}$ $\overline{14}$ $\overline{62}$ $\overline{58}$ $\overline{55}$

F. Which came first, the chicken
   or the ___? ....
   $\overline{68}$ $\overline{46}$ $\overline{52}$

G. "... through and through/the
   vorpal blade went ___!" (hyph;
   Carroll, "Jabberwocky") ....
   $\overline{13}$ $\overline{24}$ $\overline{21}$ $\overline{29}$ $\overline{8}$ $\overline{56}$ $\overline{69}$ $\overline{17}$ $\overline{65}$
   $\overline{23}$ $\overline{1}$ $\overline{49}$

H. Decay ....
   $\overline{72}$ $\overline{30}$ $\overline{6}$

I. ____ State (Ohio) ....
   $\overline{4}$ $\overline{15}$ $\overline{11}$ $\overline{12}$ $\overline{39}$ $\overline{71}$ $\overline{63}$

J. "Ali Baba and the ___ Thieves" ..
   $\overline{33}$ $\overline{26}$ $\overline{3}$ $\overline{48}$ $\overline{42}$

K. ____ behind the ears (immature,
   näive) ....
   $\overline{60}$ $\overline{5}$ $\overline{25}$

82

Y·E·A·R 1·9·2·0

1 E	2 F	3 C	4 A	5 F	6 H	7 E	8 B	9 E	■	10 A	11 C	12 F	13 B	14 D
15 E	16 E	17 A		18 C	19 F	20 B	21 A	22 E	23 G		24 G	25 E	26 D	
27 A	28 E	29 G	30 C		31 A	32 B	33 E	34 D	35 A	36 G	37 G	38 C	39 D	40 H
41 A	42 E		43 B	44 G	45 D	46 A		47 C	48 B	49 D	50 H	51 A	52 E	53 G

A. He renounced a throne for the woman he loved (name plus Roman numerals) ....
___ ___ ___ ___ ___ ___ ___ ___ ___
46 17 27 35 51 10 4 41 31
___
21

B. International agency concerned with health of children and mothers ....
___ ___ ___ ___ ___ ___
48 32 13 20 8 43

C. Rounded body; ball; area or realm ....
___ ___ ___ ___ ___ ___
30 38 47 3 18 11

D. "So, we'll go no more a ___" (from a poem by Lord Byron) .....
___ ___ ___ ___ ___ ___
26 39 45 34 49 14

E. Secret; sneaky; concealed and, usually, up to no good ....
___ ___ ___ ___ ___ ___ ___ ___ ___
1 7 25 15 33 52 42 9 28
___ ___
22 16

F. Impetuous; incautious; acting too hastily ....
___ ___ ___ ___
5 19 12 2

G. "Dirty _____" (1987 film with Swayze and Grey) ....
___ ___ ___ ___ ___ ___ ___
53 37 29 24 44 36 23

H. Aged; elderly ....
___ ___ ___
6 40 50

83

Y·E·A·R 1·9·2·6

1 G	2 K	3 C	4 I	5 A	6 A	7 E	8 K	9 A		10 D	11 C	12 B	13 A
14 I	15 C	16 L		17 J	18 H	19 I	20 K		21 B	22 C	23 F		24 A
25 B	26 K	27 J	28 I		29 L	30 C	31 G	32 B	33 H		34 D	35 A	36 G
37 E	38 C	39 F	40 G		41 L	42 J	43 I		44 G	45 A		46 B	47 K
48 I	49 D	50 D		51 C	52 F	53 K	54 D		55 B	56 E	57 H	58 A	59 F
60 C		61 E	62 D	63 C		64 G	65 K		66 K	67 L	68 D	69 B	70 J

A. Southernmost tip of South America (2 wds) ....
___ ___ ___ ___ ___ ___ ___ ___
58 5 24 35 13 45 9 6

B. Distrustful of the motives of others ....
___ ___ ___ ___ ___ ___ ___
12 32 46 25 55 21 69

C. "The Scarlet ____" (Elusive hero of novel by Baroness Orczy, 1865–1947) ....
___ ___ ___ ___ ___ ___ ___ ___ ___
63 11 3 51 38 15 22 60 30

D. Male sibling ....
___ ___ ___ ___ ___ ___ ___
34 10 62 49 50 54 68

E. Force; power ....
___ ___ ___ ___
7 56 37 61

F. All ___ (counting everyone or everything; in all) ....
___ ___ ___ ___
39 52 59 23

G. Soft, white, downy plant fibers used in making fabrics ....
___ ___ ___ ___ ___ ___
1 64 40 44 31 36

H. Not ___ behind the ears (immature; unsophisticated) .....
___ ___ ___
33 57 18

I. One who endures great suffering on behalf of a belief or cause ..
___ ___ ___ ___ ___ ___
4 14 48 28 43 19

J. Fearless, courageous, intrepid ..
___ ___ ___ ___
17 27 42 70

K. Obeyed; heeded; pursued ....
___ ___ ___ ___ ___ ___ ___ ___
65 47 26 53 2 66 8 20

L. Remove or take off, as clothing .
___ ___ ___ ___
16 67 41 29

Y·E·A·R 1·9·3·6

1 D	2 G	3 C	4 B	5 H	6 D	7 D	8 A	9 E	▪	10 G	11 H	12 H	▬	13 B
14 D	▬	15 A	16 I	17 C		18 I	19 J	20 B	21 A	22 E		23 H	24 D	25 H
26 A	27 E	28 C	29 C	30 D		31 A	32 F	33 G	34 E	35 B		36 A	37 G	
38 D	39 F	40 J	41 C	42 H		43 J	44 A	45 F	46 C	47 E	48 E		49 B	50 I
51 H	52 A	53 C	54 E	55 G		56 A	57 H	58 B	59 G	60 F	61 I	62 A	63 G	

A. "... lived a miner forty-niner and his daughter _____"; Mrs. Winston Churchill ....
   __ __ __ __ __ __ __ __ __
   31 15 62 56 26 8 44 36 21
   __
   52

B. Coalition of political parties; a thermonuclear reaction ....
   __ __ __ __ __ __
   49 20 4 13 35 58

C. ____ stick (a small rod for stirring drinks) ....
   __ __ __ __ __ __ __
   3 17 53 28 29 46 41

D. Price named as a matter of form, being trifling in comparison with actual value ....
   __ __ __ __ __ __ __
   38 30 1 7 14 24 6

E. ____ power (endurance; stamina) .
   __ __ __ __ __ __ __
   48 22 27 47 9 34 54

F. Largest continent ....
   __ __ __ __
   39 60 32 45

G. Inhabitant of Sverdlovsk or Moscow ....
   __ __ __ __ __ __ __
   63 2 10 37 59 33 55

H. Watering at the mouth, as in anticipation of food ....
   __ __ __ __ __ __ __ __
   42 51 11 5 25 57 12 23

I. Outer garment with sleeves, covering at least the upper part of the body ....
   __ __ __ __
   18 50 16 61

J. Me in Paris ....
   __ __ __
   40 19 43

85

Y·E·A·R   1·9·4·2

1 E	2 C	3 B	4 F	5 J	6 A		7 G	8 A	9 E	10 K	11 J		12 D	13 H
	14 I	15 F	16 D	17 E	18 E	19 D		20 A	21 J	22 E	23 D	24 C	25 G	26 I
	27 E	28 D	29 J	30 C		31 A	32 K		33 E	34 H	35 C	36 E	37 D	38 H
	39 J	40 B	41 A	42 E	43 H	44 J	45 E		46 G	47 A	48 B		49 E	50 J
	51 B	52 I		53 G	54 A	55 B	56 I	57 E		58 A	59 B	60 D	61 H	
62 E	63 A	64 G	65 A	66 E	67 J	68 K	69 A		70 D	71 F	72 K	73 E	74 E	75 D

A. Careful; diligent and assiduous attention to detail ....
65 54 47 58 20 31 8 6 41
69 63

B. Capital city of Croatia ....
55 51 48 40 59 3

C. Performance by one person ....
30 2 35 24

D. Baseball's Orioles play here ....
70 60 19 12 23 16 28 75 37

E. ____ who "come from a ladies' seminary" (3 wds; Gilbert and Sullivan's "The Mikado") ....
42 45 22 62 18 9 36 66 1
27 74 17 33 49 73 57

F. Gold in Mexico ....
15 4 71

G. Bay of ____ (Atlantic inlet between New Brunswick and Nova Scotia) ....
7 25 53 46 64

H. Provokes; irritates; annoys .....
61 13 43 34 38

I. Lords or gentlemen ....
26 56 14 52

J. "The maxim of the British people is '____ as usual'" (Churchill, 1914) ....
39 5 44 67 50 21 29 11

K. Spoken; vocal ....
32 72 68 10

Y·E·A·R 1·9·6·3

1 B	2 G	3 F	4 I		5 G	6 J	7 E	8 I		9 A	10 I	11 D
12 G	13 A		14 C	15 J	16 B	17 A		18 H	19 C		20 D	21 E
22 I	23 B	24 D	25 C	26 G		27 B	28 F	29 I		30 B	31 A	32 C
33 G	34 E		35 A	36 I	37 C	38 G	39 B	40 D	41 F	42 C	43 B	44 I
	45 A	46 I	47 I	48 E	49 A		50 I	51 E	52 I		53 J	54 H
55 B	56 E	57 G	58 I	59 C	60 I	61 J		62 E	63 A	64 G	65 H	66 B

A. "Sing a song of ____, a pocket full of rye" ....
<u> </u> <u> </u> <u> </u> <u> </u> <u> </u> <u> </u> <u> </u> <u> </u>
17 13 9 45 31 63 35 49

B. External boundary of an area; circumference ....
1 16 55 23 39 27 43 30 66

C. American artist famous for his "Love" poster design; his home state ....
59 42 14 32 37 19 25

D. Julius Caesar said "Veni, vidi ___" (I came, I saw, I conquered) ....
20 11 24 40

E. Set free; liberate ....
62 51 48 7 21 56 34

F. Hawaiian dish made from taro root ....
3 41 28

G. Bellicose chauvinism, favoring an aggressive foreign policy ....
5 64 26 33 2 12 57 38

H. Deal a blow; reach a specified level ....
54 18 65

I. "... but in this world nothing is certain but ____" (3 wds; Benjamin Franklin) ....
44 4 60 22 36 50 8 52 58
47 10 46 29

J. Penny, nickel, dime or quarter ..
53 6 15 61

87

Y·E·A·R 1·9·7·2

		1 E	2 C	3 C	4 B	–	5 A	6 D	7 D	8 A		9 F	10 H
11 E	12 A	13 F	14 G	15 C		16 A	17 H	18 A	19 A	20 D	21 E	22 B	23 F
	24 E	25 I	26 I	27 A	28 D	29 A	30 B		31 H	32 A	33 D	34 B	35 E
36 C	37 H	38 A		39 F	40 E		41 A	42 G	43 F	44 D	45 A	46 I	
47 C	48 I		49 A	50 D	51 C		52 H	53 B	54 D	55 G	56 A		

A. Marie Antoinette supposedly said this (4 wds) ....
32 38 12 5 56 27 19 45 49
29 16 18 41 8

B. "... wherefore art thou ____?" asks Juliet ....
53 22 34 4 30

C. He wrote "The Legend of Sleepy Hollow" ....
2 51 3 47 36 15

D. Of or befitting an emperor; of a commanding manner; domineering
6 7 20 33 28 50 54 44

E. Conflict, discord, or antagonism; competition or rivalry ....
40 11 24 21 1 35

F. Small Russian pancake, usually served with caviar ....
9 43 13 23 39

G. Gluttony or sloth, for example ..
55 42 14

H. "____-22" (Joseph Heller's WWII novel) ....
31 10 37 52 17

I. Ian Fleming hero ....
26 25 48 46

Y·E·A·R 1·9·7·4

1 E	2 J	3 F	4 D		5 B	6 D	7 C	8 G	9 A		10 H	11 H	12 J	13 A
14 B	15 I		16 C	17 E		18 F	19 A	20 C	21 E	22 B		23 F	24 C	25 H
26 G	27 F	28 C		29 H	30 A	31 H	32 I	33 B	34 F	35 D	36 A	37 J		38 C
39 D	40 E	41 J	42 C	43 G	44 A	45 H	46 H		47 J	48 B	49 B	50 C	51 J	52 H
53 G		54 D	55 I	56 B		57 H	58 F	59 H	60 C	61 H	62 A	63 A	64 E	

A. Washington's NFL team ....
    30 63 13 44 62 19 36 9

B. Nazi field marshal (1893–1946), he headed Luftwaffe ....
    5 14 48 56 33 22 49

C. Gregarious; interested in things outside the self ....
    38 20 16 50 24 7 42 28 60

D. Firmly fastened; intent upon something ....
    54 6 39 35 4

E. Light and good-humored imitation of something ....
    64 40 17 21 1

F. Quaker ....
    23 3 58 27 18 34

G. Predicament; muddle; untidy condition ....
    26 8 43 53

H. American who won 1990 U.S. Open tennis title (full name) ....
    29 45 52 31 59 11 57 10 25
    61 46

I. Male child in relation to his parents ....
    32 55 15

J. Intense fear; horror; panic .....
    37 51 12 47 2 41

Y·E·A·R 1·9·7·4

1 I	2 H	3 K	4 K	5 J	6 E	7 J		8 A	9 J	10 D	11 E	12 D	
13 B	14 H	15 A	16 C	17 B	18 A		19 E	20 F	21 J	22 G	23 C		24 H
25 B	26 I	27 G	28 E		29 A	30 C	31 G	32 E		33 C	34 J	35 K	36 E
37 J	38 F	39 B	40 A	41 B		42 B	43 G	44 C	45 F	46 A	47 K	48 B	49 C
	50 I	51 A		52 B	53 G	54 C	55 I	56 D	57 J	58 B	59 A	60 B	61 F

A. Country on the northern border
   of South Africa ....
   ‾29‾ ‾51‾ ‾59‾ ‾18‾ ‾46‾ ‾40‾ ‾8‾ ‾15‾

B. "Hiawatha" poet (1807–82) ....
   ‾48‾ ‾60‾ ‾39‾ ‾58‾ ‾42‾ ‾17‾ ‾13‾ ‾41‾ ‾25‾
                                                   ‾52‾

C. Slavishly submissive; fawning;
   abject ....
   ‾54‾ ‾23‾ ‾44‾ ‾16‾ ‾30‾ ‾49‾ ‾33‾

D. Veto; prohibit ....
   ‾12‾ ‾56‾ ‾10‾

E. Babel and Pisa ....
   ‾36‾ ‾11‾ ‾19‾ ‾28‾ ‾6‾ ‾32‾

F. Fine-textured whetstone for
   sharpening razors ....
   ‾20‾ ‾38‾ ‾61‾ ‾45‾

G. Egyptian president assassinated
   in 1981 ....
   ‾27‾ ‾43‾ ‾31‾ ‾53‾ ‾22‾

H. Go in haste ....
   ‾24‾ ‾2‾ ‾14‾

I. Baseball's Bambino ....
   ‾1‾ ‾26‾ ‾50‾ ‾55‾

J. He ruled Uganda harshly from
   1971 to 1979 (full name) ....
   ‾37‾ ‾7‾ ‾21‾ ‾5‾ ‾34‾ ‾9‾ ‾57‾

K. Nymph who pined away for love
   of Narcissus until only her
   voice remained ....
   ‾47‾ ‾3‾ ‾4‾ ‾35‾

Y·E·A·R 1·9·7·4

1 A	2 E	3 H	4 G	5 B	6 A		7 A	8 C	9 A	10 D	11 H		12 G
13 C	14 B	15 F	16 G		17 G	18 A	19 F	20 G	21 B		22 G	23 A	
24 B	25 D	26 E	27 D	28 C	29 A		30 B	31 G	32 E	33 D	34 G		35 H
36 H	37 F	38 C	39 A	40 B	41 H	42 C	43 H	44 B		45 A	46 G	47 E	48 H
	49 A	50 G	51 G	52 D	53 E	54 A	55 F		56 D	57 C	58 B	59 A	

A. Penn State football team (2 wds)
$\overline{23}\ \overline{45}\ \overline{1}\ \overline{39}\ \overline{59}\ \overline{9}\ \overline{6}\ \overline{7}\ \overline{54}$
$\overline{18}\ \overline{49}\ \overline{29}$

B. German automobile brand ....
$\overline{14}\ \overline{58}\ \overline{40}\ \overline{24}\ \overline{5}\ \overline{30}\ \overline{21}\ \overline{44}$

C. Ancient Roman goddess of the dawn ....
$\overline{8}\ \overline{28}\ \overline{13}\ \overline{42}\ \overline{57}\ \overline{38}$

D. Humorous or satirical imitation of a person, event, or writing ..
$\overline{33}\ \overline{56}\ \overline{27}\ \overline{52}\ \overline{10}\ \overline{25}$

E. Issue forth with force, as liquid through a narrow orifice .
$\overline{53}\ \overline{26}\ \overline{32}\ \overline{2}\ \overline{47}$

F. Unusual; extraordinary; cooked just slightly ....
$\overline{37}\ \overline{55}\ \overline{19}\ \overline{15}$

G. Best-selling English author of novels with horseracing background (full name) ....
$\overline{16}\ \overline{22}\ \overline{51}\ \overline{4}\ \overline{17}\ \overline{31}\ \overline{12}\ \overline{46}\ \overline{20}$
$\overline{50}\ \overline{34}$

H. With reference; opportune; pertinent ....
$\overline{36}\ \overline{43}\ \overline{3}\ \overline{48}\ \overline{35}\ \overline{41}\ \overline{11}$

91

Y·E·A·R 1·9·7·4

	1 B	2 C	3 E	4 A	5 F	6 G	7 E		8 D	9 A	10 H	11 C
12 B		13 A	14 E	15 D	16 F		17 B	18 A	19 A	20 G	21 B	22 C
23 E		24 F	25 H	26 G	27 H	28 A		29 H	30 F	31 C	32 B	33 A
	34 H	35 C	36 G	37 E	38 F		39 A	40 B		41 A	42 I	43 D
44 B	45 E	46 H	47 C	48 D	49 H		50 I	51 A	52 B	53 H	54 F	55 D
56 I	57 A	58 C	59 D		60 B	61 A	62 H	63 E	64 C	65 B	66 A	

A. Vice-president who became president when Lincoln was shot (full name) 57 28 19 9 4 41 13 51 61

33 66 39 18

B. Full trust; self-reliance, assurance 60 32 40 1 17 12 44 52 21

65

C. Unduly demanding; difficult; requiring great skill or care ... 2 31 47 58 22 35 11 64

D. Plucky; resolute and courageous . 8 15 55 48 43 59

E. Passed over lightly; pronounced indistinctly; slandered 23 7 14 63 45 37 3

F. Excessively proper; prim 54 5 30 24 38 16

G. Distinguished female singer; prima donna 36 20 26 6

H. Body of water between Greece and Turkey (2 wds) 10 25 46 49 62 29 53 27 34

I. Part of elevator that carries the passengers or freight 50 42 56

92

Y·E·A·R 2·2·4·B·C

		1 I	2 B	3 A	4 B	5 B		6 H	7 E	8 D	9 B	10 G	11 A
	12 C	13 H		14 D	15 G	16 B		17 A	18 E	19 E		20 B	21 C
22 A	23 H	24 G	25 D	26 E	27 B		28 G	29 F		30 A	31 C	32 E	33 A
34 B	35 F		36 A	37 H	38 B	39 G	40 A	41 H	42 I	43 G	44 D		45 B
46 A		47 B	48 F	49 G	50 F	51 B	52 G	53 G	54 I	55 C	56 B		

A. Paul Simon's 1987 best record Grammy ....
$\overline{17}\ \overline{30}\ \overline{40}\ \overline{36}\ \overline{11}\ \overline{22}\ \overline{3}\ \overline{46}\ \overline{33}$

B. Vaduz is the capital of this tiny principality between Austria and Switzerland ....
$\overline{38}\ \overline{45}\ \overline{56}\ \overline{20}\ \overline{51}\ \overline{9}\ \overline{34}\ \overline{16}\ \overline{27}$
$\overline{5}\ \overline{47}\ \overline{2}\ \overline{4}$

C. His nemesis was Peter Pan ....
$\overline{31}\ \overline{21}\ \overline{12}\ \overline{55}$

D. Impudent or disrespectful back talk (informal) ....
$\overline{25}\ \overline{8}\ \overline{44}\ \overline{14}$

E. Surpass in execution or performance ....
$\overline{18}\ \overline{26}\ \overline{7}\ \overline{19}\ \overline{32}$

F. Waller of "Ain't Misbehavin'" and "Honeysuckle Rose" ....
$\overline{29}\ \overline{48}\ \overline{50}\ \overline{35}$

G. Complaining; grumbling; petulant; discontented ....
$\overline{52}\ \overline{10}\ \overline{43}\ \overline{49}\ \overline{15}\ \overline{39}\ \overline{28}\ \overline{53}\ \overline{24}$

H. Mocking imitation of someone or something, usually light and good-humored ....
$\overline{6}\ \overline{41}\ \overline{37}\ \overline{23}\ \overline{13}$

I. Step on the ___ (hurry) ....
$\overline{1}\ \overline{54}\ \overline{42}$

93

Y·E·A·R 4·6·0·B·C

1 C	2 A	3 G	4 G	5 F	6 A	7 D	8 H	9 B	10 D		11 A	12 B	13 E
14 F	15 G		16 C	17 B	18 A	19 F	20 C		21 H	22 G	23 D		24 A
25 B	26 E	27 B	28 G	29 E	30 A	31 C	32 B		33 E	34 A	35 D	36 G	37 F
	38 C	39 B		40 H	41 G	42 G	43 D	44 A		45 H	46 B	47 E	

A. He played the Cowardly Lion
(full name) .... ― ― ― ― ― ― ― ―
11 18 34 6 30 24 44 2

B. Deceptively plausible or
attractive; misleading .... ― ― ― ― ― ― ― ―
32 17 25 27 46 12 9 39

C. Devout; godly; reverent .... ― ― ― ― ―
1 38 16 31 20

D. Novelist Irwin and dramatist
George Bernard .... ― ― ― ― ―
43 7 35 23 10

E. Burn the midnight oil .... ― ― ― ― ―
26 47 13 33 29

F. Queen of Great Britain
(1702-14) and last of the
Stuart monarchs .... ― ― ― ―
37 14 19 5

G. Founder of Islam .... ― ― ― ― ― ― ― ―
4 3 28 42 36 41 22 15

H. Females of the domestic fowl .... ― ― ― ―
45 8 21 40

Y·E·A·R 5·4·B·C

1 B	2 D	3 C	4 D	5 A	6 H	7 B		8 C	9 C	10 F	11 F	12 A	13 G
14 C	15 A		16 B	17 H		18 A	19 F	20 E	21 E		22 D	23 A	24 B
	25 F	26 A	27 E	28 B	29 D	30 D	31 G	32 B		33 C	34 A		35 D
36 A	37 G	38 H		39 E	40 B	41 G	42 H	43 F	44 H	45 C	46 D	47 A	

A. Woody Allen's 1987 film about
the '30s broadcast era (2 wds) ··
$\overline{5}$ $\overline{47}$ $\overline{18}$ $\overline{36}$ $\overline{26}$ $\overline{12}$ $\overline{23}$ $\overline{34}$ $\overline{15}$

B. Stray from the main subject;
ramble ·························
$\overline{32}$ $\overline{16}$ $\overline{40}$ $\overline{7}$ $\overline{1}$ $\overline{24}$ $\overline{28}$

C. Go ___ (issue stock for sale) ···
$\overline{3}$ $\overline{14}$ $\overline{33}$ $\overline{9}$ $\overline{45}$ $\overline{8}$

D. "... from the fields there
comes the scent of ____ hay"
(hyph) ·························
$\overline{46}$ $\overline{4}$ $\overline{35}$ $\overline{2}$ $\overline{29}$ $\overline{22}$ $\overline{30}$

E. Verdi's 1871 opera, set in
ancient Egypt ··················
$\overline{20}$ $\overline{27}$ $\overline{21}$ $\overline{39}$

F. Insects in the transformation
stage between larva and adult ···
$\overline{25}$ $\overline{11}$ $\overline{43}$ $\overline{10}$ $\overline{19}$

G. Play with ___ (trifle with a
serious or dangerous matter) ····
$\overline{37}$ $\overline{13}$ $\overline{41}$ $\overline{31}$

H. Composure; dignified
self-confident manner ···········
$\overline{44}$ $\overline{6}$ $\overline{42}$ $\overline{17}$ $\overline{38}$

95

Y·E·A·R 1·7·1·8

1 F	2 A	3 E	4 C	5 B	6 G	7 H	8 C	9 B	10 F		11 J	12 D	13 C
	14 I	15 B	16 E	17 C	18 K	19 J		20 I	21 B		22 J	23 K	24 A
25 D	26 C	27 H		28 G	29 F		30 C	31 A	32 D		33 C	34 I	35 H
36 D		37 J	38 A		39 C	40 D	41 E	42 F	43 J		44 G	45 G	
46 K	47 A	48 F	49 C	50 J	51 D	52 E		53 A	54 I	55 C	56 J	57 F

A. "In your Easter bonnet, with all the ___ upon it" (from an Irving Berlin song) ....
<u>53</u> <u>47</u> <u>31</u> <u>2</u> <u>24</u> <u>38</u>

B. Exposure to the chance of injury or loss; peril ....
<u>9</u> <u>15</u> <u>21</u> <u>5</u>

C. "A Day ____" (3 wds; Marx Brothers film) ....
<u>17</u> <u>49</u> <u>39</u> <u>30</u> <u>13</u> <u>55</u> <u>8</u> <u>4</u> <u>26</u>
<u>33</u>

D. Tom Hanks met mermaid Daryl Hannah in this 1984 film ....
<u>32</u> <u>36</u> <u>25</u> <u>40</u> <u>51</u> <u>12</u>

E. Listen! ....
<u>52</u> <u>3</u> <u>16</u> <u>41</u>

F. Near; next to; compared with; apart from ....
<u>1</u> <u>57</u> <u>29</u> <u>48</u> <u>10</u> <u>42</u>

G. Treat gently; pamper ....
<u>44</u> <u>28</u> <u>6</u> <u>45</u>

H. The ___ is cast (the irrevocable decision has been made) ....
<u>27</u> <u>35</u> <u>7</u>

I. Member of a Pueblo Indian people of northern Arizona ......
<u>34</u> <u>54</u> <u>14</u> <u>20</u>

J. Pertaining to or caused by motion ....
<u>22</u> <u>50</u> <u>43</u> <u>19</u> <u>11</u> <u>37</u> <u>56</u>

K. Single basic unit of computer information ....
<u>46</u> <u>23</u> <u>18</u>

Y·E·A·R 1·9·2·7

		1 C	2 A	3 I	4 J	5 G		6 D	7 C	8 G	9 E		10 D	11 B
	12 A	13 C	14 I	15 G	16 H	17 G	18 C		19 A	20 B	21 D	22 F	23 A	24 G
25 G	26 G	27 G		28 I	29 D	30 F	31 B	32 A		33 G	34 E	35 H	36 A	37 B
38 I	39 E	40 G		41 J	42 A	43 I	44 B	45 D	46 A	47 A		48 F	49 D	
50 A	51 B	52 F	53 J	54 I		55 H	56 E	57 B	58 G	59 I	60 D	61 J		62 A
63 B	64 H	65 C		66 A	67 E	68 D		69 H	70 G	71 I	72 G	73 B		

A. Surrealist painter of 1937 anti-war canvas "Guernica" (full name) ....

$\overline{50}\ \overline{36}\ \overline{23}\ \overline{19}\ \overline{46}\ \overline{47}\ \overline{2}\ \overline{12}\ \overline{66}$

$\overline{62}\ \overline{32}\ \overline{42}$

B. Temporary; lasting only a short time ....

$\overline{73}\ \overline{57}\ \overline{51}\ \overline{37}\ \overline{44}\ \overline{20}\ \overline{31}\ \overline{63}\ \overline{11}$

C. Utters a loud, prolonged, mournful cry, as that of a dog or wolf ....

$\overline{13}\ \overline{7}\ \overline{65}\ \overline{1}\ \overline{18}$

D. Moving with short, unsteady steps, as a child ....

$\overline{45}\ \overline{49}\ \overline{68}\ \overline{6}\ \overline{29}\ \overline{10}\ \overline{21}\ \overline{60}$

E. Makes indirect suggestion or allusion; intimates ....

$\overline{56}\ \overline{39}\ \overline{67}\ \overline{34}\ \overline{9}$

F. To dish the ____ (to gossip maliciously) ....

$\overline{22}\ \overline{30}\ \overline{52}\ \overline{48}$

G. US journalist (1811-1872), he advised "Go west, young man" (full name) ....

$\overline{27}\ \overline{58}\ \overline{15}\ \overline{33}\ \overline{40}\ \overline{72}\ \overline{26}\ \overline{25}\ \overline{8}$

$\overline{17}\ \overline{70}\ \overline{24}\ \overline{5}$

H. "... never send to know for whom the bell ___" (Donne, "Devotions upon Emergent Occasions") ....

$\overline{55}\ \overline{64}\ \overline{16}\ \overline{35}\ \overline{69}$

I. Detach ....

$\overline{59}\ \overline{43}\ \overline{28}\ \overline{14}\ \overline{54}\ \overline{38}\ \overline{71}\ \overline{3}$

J. Sir Francis Drake sailed around the world aboard the "Golden ___" ....

$\overline{61}\ \overline{53}\ \overline{41}\ \overline{4}$

Y·E·A·R 1·7·7·0

1 F	2 B	3 D	4 C	5 B	6 E	7 F		8 H	9 H	10 G	11 A	12 F	13 H	14 H
15 D		16 B	17 C	18 F	19 E		20 A	21 C		22 D	23 C	24 A	25 C	26 E
27 B	28 F	29 A	30 C		31 A	32 F	33 F		34 G	35 A	36 B	37 E	38 G	39 A
	40 F	41 F	42 C	43 F	44 A	45 F	46 C	47 B	48 E	49 H		50 F	51 E	
52 A	53 C	54 D	55 F	56 A	57 C		58 F	59 A	60 D	61 F	62 B	63 H	64 A	65 D

A. He refused the 1972 best actor Oscar for "The Godfather" (full name) ....
31 59 64 35 20 39 52 24 44
29 11 56

B. Tinker Bell was one of them; pixies; leprechauns ....
16 62 5 2 47 36 27

C. Inactivity; motionless state ....
42 46 25 30 57 23 4 17 53
21

D. Makes a catlike sound to express disapproval or contempt .
22 3 60 54 65 15

E. You win if you keep hitting these on a first roll of the dice ....
6 48 37 19 51 26

F. Canadian province bordering on Washington, Idaho, and Montana (2 wds) ....
33 18 28 55 12 61 7 40 32
45 43 58 1 50 41

G. "Light Horse Harry" or his Civil War general son ....
10 34 38

H. A great many; groups of twenty ..
49 63 9 14 13 8

98

Y·E·A·R   1·8·6·1

	1 G	2 H	3 F	4 D	5 A	6 A	7 D	8 C	9 B		10 D	11 G	12 H
13 F	14 E		15 D	16 F		17 G	18 B	19 E	20 D	21 F		22 B	23 A
24 D	25 F	26 G	27 H	28 A	29 D	30 B	31 D	32 G		33 A	34 G	35 G	36 E
37 D	38 B	39 D	40 A	41 D		42 C	43 H	44 B	45 F	46 G	47 D	48 A	49 B
50 C	51 B		52 A	53 B		54 B	55 C	56 D	57 E	58 A	59 F	60 A	

A. State capital of Vermont ....
　48　23　40　58　33　28　60　52　5
　6

B. Supremacy; domination; command ..
　18　53　22　49　9　38　30　44　54
　51

C. Love in Mexico ....
　55　42　8　50

D. 1991 film starring Nick Nolte and Barbra Streisand (3 wds) .,...
　56　29　37　24　31　20　47　4　41
　15　10　39　7

E. A ___ is as good as a mile (it's the same if one loses by a lot or by a little) ....
　19　57　36　14

F. Pertaining to a woman; female ...
　21　13　16　45　59　3　25

G. Lady ____ (queen of England for 9 days in 1553, then beheaded; full name) ....
　1　11　17　35　46　34　26　32

H. It returned to the ark with a fresh olive leaf in its mouth ...
　27　43　12　2

99

Y·E·A·R 1·9·7·0

	1 A	2 A	3 H	4 B	5 C	6 B	7 I		8 E	9 A	10 G	11 A
12 C	13 C	14 E	15 D		16 A	17 F	18 G	19 E	20 A	21 C	22 H	
23 B	24 F		25 A	26 E	27 I	28 C	29 B	30 D	31 A		32 E	33 E
	34 C	35 G	36 A		37 F	38 H	39 H	40 G	41 C	42 A	43 D	44 I
45 C	46 B		47 F	48 H		49 I	50 E	51 D	52 F	53 G		

A. First family (3 wds) .... __ __ __ __ __ __ __ __ __
                                      2 42 16 1 9 20 31 36 11
                                                              __
                                                              25

B. In Roman numerals it's LX .... __ __ __ __ __
                                      6 23 4 29 46

C. Intended to teach; morally
   instructive; pedantic .... __ __ __ __ __ __ __ __
                                     21 5 13 12 28 34 41 45

D. Cleveland is on this Great Lake . __ __ __ __
                                     30 15 51 43

E. Landlocked kingdom, formerly
   Basutoland, surrounded by South
   Africa .... __ __ __ __ __ __ __
                                    26 19 8 33 32 50 14

F. Place to go on Election Day ..... __ __ __ __ __
                                     37 47 17 52 24

G. Light, long, narrow racing boat
   for rowing by one or more
   persons .... __ __ __ __ __
                                    40 35 53 10 18

H. Enjoying more liberty or
   political independence than
   others .... __ __ __ __ __
                                    48 3 39 22 38

I. One-tenth of a dime .... __ __ __ __
                                    49 27 44 7

100

Y·E·A·R 1·9·8·6

		1 A	2 H	3 F	4 J	5 E	6 B	7 I	8 J	9 A	10 C	11 E		12 D
13 F	14 B	15 F	16 G	17 I	18 H		19 D	20 J	21 B	22 A		23 C	24 J	25 G
26 B	27 D	28 G	29 F	30 D	31 A		32 B	33 D	34 E	35 C	36 H	37 I	38 J	39 J
	40 C	41 B		42 E	43 J	44 A	45 H	46 D	47 F	48 C	49 I	50 G		51 J
52 B	53 A	54 G		55 F	56 B	57 H	58 H		59 C	60 E	61 B	62 D		

A. His first novel was "The Naked and the Dead" (1948) ....
___ ___ ___ ___ ___ ___
22 44 9 31 53 1

B. 1985 western film with Kevins Kline and Costner ....
___ ___ ___ ___ ___ ___ ___ ___ ___
41 56 14 52 61 26 6 32 21

C. Roe of sturgeon, especially the beluga ....
___ ___ ___ ___ ___ ___
23 35 10 40 59 48

D. She had a 1987 hit single, "I Think We're Alone Now" ....
___ ___ ___ ___ ___ ___ ___
46 33 12 19 62 27 30

E. Wars of the ___ (intermittent struggle for the English throne, 1455-1485) ....
___ ___ ___ ___ ___
60 5 42 11 34

F. Cried or wailed lustily ....
___ ___ ___ ___ ___ ___
29 13 55 15 47 3

G. Public exhibition of cowboy skills, such as bronco riding and calf roping ....
___ ___ ___ ___ ___
54 16 50 25 28

H. Declared definitely or specifically; asserted ....
___ ___ ___ ___ ___ ___
36 18 2 45 58 57

I. Pleasingly pretty or dainty, as a child or a hat ....
___ ___ ___ ___
7 17 37 49

J. Art of formal speaking or writing; inflated discourse .....
___ ___ ___ ___ ___ ___ ___ ___
20 24 38 8 51 39 4 43

A N S W E R S

1

HEADLINE: MONTEZUMA GREETS CORTES
AS WHITE GOD QUETZALCOATL.

YEAR: 1519

ANSWERS:

A. Michelangelo	**D.** Astute	**G.** Quart
B. Zest	**E.** Great	**H.** Doze
C. Cow	**F.** Toms	

2

HEADLINE: ALEXANDER THE GREAT IS DEAD IN BABYLON
AT THE AGE OF THIRTY-THREE.

YEAR: 323 BC

ANSWERS:

A. Dirty Harry	**D.** Tea	**G.** Hexagon
B. Balboa	**E.** Helena	**H.** Teeth
C. Fetter	**F.** Staid	**I.** Deign

3

HEADLINE: BEAUREGARD'S CONFEDERATE TROOPS
ATTACK FORT SUMTER. WAR BEGINS.

YEAR: 1861

ANSWERS:

A. Art Deco	**D.** Untoward	**G.** Feast
B. George	**E.** Brunt	**H.** Packers
C. Miser	**F.** After	**I.** Boats

4

HEADLINE: KHRUSHCHEV AGREES TO RETURN
CUBAN MISSILES TO RUSSIA.

YEAR: 1962

ANSWERS:

A. Kim Carnes	**D.** Recant	**G.** Hugh
B. Burts	**E.** Suits	**H.** Suave
C. Horse	**F.** Oilers	

5

HEADLINE: ALLIED FIGHTER-BOMBERS POUND IRAQ
WITH RECORD NUMBER OF MISSIONS.

YEAR: 1991

ANSWERS:

A. League of Nations	**D.** Sword	**G.** Perth
B. Relinquish	**E.** Mice	**H.** Bib
C. Birds	**F.** Form	**I.** Dorm

6

HEADLINE: BATISTA FLEES CUBA. FIDEL CASTRO TAKES HAVANA AND ESTABLISHES NEW GOVERNMENT.

YEAR: 1959

ANSWERS:

A. Relevant	E. Nile	I. Wise
B. Oakland	F. Heaven's Gate	J. Sadat
C. Chaff	G. Mess	K. Base
D. Stubborn	H. Attic	

7

HEADLINE: PAUL REVERE RIDES FROM BOSTON TO LEXINGTON TO WARN OF BRITISH ADVANCE.

YEAR: 1775

ANSWERS:

A. Batmobile	E. Norton	H. Feverish
B. Pinnacle	F. Wavering	I. Dour
C. Texas	G. Rot	J. Sot
D. Ford		

8

HEADLINE: CHURCHILL AND ROOSEVELT MEET IN CASABLANCA TO SET ALLIED STRATEGY.

YEAR: 1943

ANSWERS:

A. Sesame Street	D. Itty	G. Accolade
B. Cardinals	E. The Love Boat	H. Clan
C. Ring	F. Hull	

9

HEADLINE: CATHEDRAL OF COLOGNE IS COMPLETED. TOOK MORE THAN SIX HUNDRED YEARS.

YEAR: 1880

ANSWERS:

A. A thousand ships	D. Ode	G. Helen of Troy
B. Carroll	E. Deck	H. Nog
C. Extricate	F. Modem	

10

HEADLINE: ISRAELIS ROUT THE ARABS. OCCUPY OLD CITY OF JERUSALEM. SWEEP THROUGH SINAI TOWARDS SUEZ CANAL.

YEAR: 1967

ANSWERS:

A. Tom Cruise	E. Warp	I. Raw
B. Laissez faire	F. Slay	J. Chocolate
C. Obtuse	G. Ash	K. July
D. Praised	H. Our discontent	L. Hug

11

HEADLINE: ETHAN ALLEN'S GREEN MOUNTAIN BOYS SEIZE BRITISH FORT AT TICONDEROGA.

YEAR: 1775

ANSWERS:

A. From Here to Eternity
B. Austin
C. Stage
D. Barbizon
E. Lead
F. Nicholson
G. Gin
H. Seat

12

HEADLINE: BATISTA CRUSHES ABORTIVE REVOLUTION AND IMPRISONS LEADER FIDEL CASTRO.

YEAR: 1953

ANSWERS:

A. Treasure Island
B. Poseidon
C. Dover
D. Snails
E. Bravo
F. Curie
G. Static
H. Far
I. Blithe
J. Tom

13

HEADLINE: FLOOD FINALLY RECEDES. NOAH'S ARK LANDS UPON THE MOUNTAINS OF ARARAT.

YEAR: Biblical

ANSWERS:

A. Don Shula
B. Napa
C. Crony
D. The Killers
E. Fatalist
F. Offer
G. Adorn
H. Amadeus
I. Noon

14

HEADLINE: ALBERT OF SAXE-COBURG MARRIES QUEEN VICTORIA. BECOMES PRINCE CONSORT OF ENGLAND.

YEAR: 1840

ANSWERS:

A. Connors
B. Axis
C. Rosebuds
D. Grace
E. Facet
F. Quote
G. Feeble
H. Crab
I. Prime time
J. Loon
K. Craving
L. Nor

15

HEADLINE: ENGLISH FORCES UNDER HENRY V ROUT THE FRENCH ARMY AT AGINCOURT.

YEAR: 1415

ANSWERS:

A. Mercy
B. Forage
C. Heart
D. Streisand
E. Vent
F. Cher
G. Funny
H. Girl
I. Huron
J. Touch

16

HEADLINE: CHURCHILL, ROOSEVELT AND CHIANG MEET IN CAIRO. SET TERMS FOR JAPAN'S DEFEAT.

YEAR: 1943

ANSWERS:

A. Scandinavia	D. Emulate	G. Christmas
B. Clifford	E. Renege	H. Sloth
C. Tojo	F. Thee	I. Prancer

17

HEADLINE: BENAZIR BHUTTO IS NAMED FIRST WOMAN PRIME MINISTER OF PAKISTAN.

YEAR: 1988

ANSWERS:

A. Fantasia	D. Wok	G. Mist
B. Prime time	E. Iris	H. Bonanza
C. Foment	F. Hepburns	I. Dirt

18

HEADLINE: IRAQIS FIRE SCUD MISSILES AT ISRAEL. HIT TEL AVIV AND HAIFA.

YEAR: 1991

ANSWERS:

A. Rehnquist	D. Davis	G. Asiatic
B. Lavish	E. Familiar	H. Tea
C. Fliers	F. Side	

19

HEADLINE: CAESAR DEAD. CONSPIRATOR CASSIUS FLEES TO SYRIA WITH HIS ARMY.

YEAR: 44 BC

ANSWERS:

A. Aretha	D. Adroit	G. Cry
B. Saucer	E. Few	H. Raisa
C. Coop	F. Miles Standish	I. Sissy

20

HEADLINE: ITALY SURRENDERS UNCONDITIONALLY. ARMISTICE SIGNED. ALLIED TROOPS LAND IN NAPLES AREA.

YEAR: 1943

ANSWERS:

A. A la carte	E. Tell	H. Denying
B. Supercilious	F. Strained	I. Error
C. And no man	G. Tidy	J. Sells
D. Indianapolis		

21

HEADLINE: ARMY OF ALEXANDER OF MACEDONIA CROSSES THE HELLESPONT AND WARS ON PERSIA.

YEAR: 334 BC

ANSWERS:

A. Walt Disney	E. Noose	I. Merrier
B. Aloha	F. Par	J. Ascent
C. Exact	G. Flanders	K. Spoon
D. Foam	H. She	

22

HEADLINE: REVELATION PROPHESIES POWERS OF GOOD WILL DESTROY FORCES OF EVIL AT ARMAGEDDON.

YEAR: Biblical

ANSWERS:

A. Chris Evert	E. Mary Poppins	I. Goo
B. Eagles	F. Ides	J. Stored
C. Fervor	G. Wail	K. Woolf
D. Date	H. Eon	L. Flood

23

HEADLINE: NAPOLEON'S ARMY DEFEATS COMBINED AUSTRIAN AND RUSSIAN FORCES AT AUSTERLITZ.

YEAR: 1805

ANSWERS:

A. Treasure Island	D. Amorous	G. Pace
B. Fail-safe	E. Tint	H. Understand
C. Cozy	F. Bannister	I. Amos

24

HEADLINE: JIMMY CARTER OF GEORGIA WINS DEMOCRATIC PRESIDENTIAL NOMINATION.

YEAR: 1976

ANSWERS:

A. Perry Mason	E. Fit	H. Indigo
B. Ironic	F. Andrew Carnegie	I. Tic
C. Mamas	G. Mil	J. Joe
D. Tot		

25

HEADLINE: DOW JONES INDUSTRIALS PLUNGE OVER FIVE HUNDRED POINTS ON BLACK MONDAY.

YEAR: 1987

ANSWERS:

A. Once upon a time	D. Around the World	G. Fiend
B. Savvy	E. Jobs	H. Sod
C. Drunken	F. Spilling	

26

HEADLINE: ROMAN ARMY ENDS PUNIC WARS BY RAZING CARTHAGE TO THE GROUND.

YEAR: 146 BC

ANSWERS:

A. What's up doc
B. Byron
C. Arizona
D. Chang
E. Rags
F. Rudimentary
G. Germ
H. Net

27

HEADLINE: WORLD BANK IS ESTABLISHED AT BRETTON WOODS UNITED NATIONS CONFERENCE.

YEAR: 1944

ANSWERS:

A. A Tale of Two Cities
B. Beset
C. Whacks
D. Banner
E. Din
F. Turned
G. Ono
H. Blonde
I. Dross
J. Tin

28

HEADLINE: BUFFALO BILL WILD WEST SHOW TOURS EUROPE TO INTERNATIONAL ACCLAIM.

YEAR: 1873

ANSWERS:

A. Last straw
B. Preclude
C. Curious
D. Wan
E. Anon
F. William Tell
G. Fit
H. Boo-boo
I. Thief

29

HEADLINE: TOLEDO ALCAZAR CONTINUES TO HOLD OUT AGAINST SIEGE BY FALANGIST FORCES.

YEAR: 1936

ANSWERS:

A. Bahrain
B. Goofy
C. Dozen
D. Instigate
E. Good
F. Uncle
G. Closet
H. Australia
I. Soft
J. Cleats

30

HEADLINE: YACHTSMAN FRANCIS CHICHESTER COMPLETES SOLO VOYAGE AROUND THE WORLD.

YEAR: 1967

ANSWERS:

A. Crystal Palace
B. Tout
C. Choo-choo
D. Whys
E. Sins
F. Love Me Tender
G. Framed
H. Char
I. Sing

31

HEADLINE: POMP AND CEREMONY AS PRINCE CHARLES MARRIES LADY DIANA SPENCER.

YEAR: 1981

ANSWERS:

A. Deerslayer
B. Morose
C. Prince
D. Al Capp
E. Manic
F. Sandy
G. Price
H. Dasher
I. Mann

32

HEADLINE: WORK BEGINS ON CHANNEL TUNNEL. WILL RUN FROM FOLKESTONE TO CALAIS.

YEAR: 1987

ANSWERS:

A. Colosseum
B. Flintstone
C. Libel
D. Wankel
E. Crank
F. North
G. Fooling
H. Nun
I. Ware

33

HEADLINE: SERPENT CONVINCES EVE TO EAT APPLE. BOTH SHE AND ADAM ARE BANISHED FROM GARDEN OF EDEN.

YEAR: Biblical

ANSWERS:

A. Geppetto
B. And peasant slave
C. Vehemence
D. Coded
E. Hen
F. Fantasia
G. Bon
H. Freedom
I. Bred
J. Harrison

34

HEADLINE: JAPAN SURRENDERS UNCONDITIONALLY. SIGNS RIGID TERMS IN CEREMONY ON WARSHIP MISSOURI.

YEAR: 1945

ANSWERS:

A. Juneau
B. Lean and hungry
C. Pomposity
D. Crisis
E. Wilderness
F. Nor
G. Missing in action
H. Red
I. Mirrors

35

HEADLINE: SUPREME COURT HOLDS THAT SEPARATE BUT EQUAL PUBLIC EDUCATION HAS NO PLACE.

YEAR: 1954

ANSWERS:

A. The Muppets
B. Coalesced
C. Houdini
D. Plata
E. Bar
F. Capulet
G. Hunt
H. Close quarters
I. Abou

36

HEADLINE: GIANTS' WILLIE MAYS BELTS FIFTY-SECOND ROUND-TRIPPER OF SEASON. WINS HOME RUN CROWN.

YEAR: 1965

ANSWERS:

A. Nancy	E. Brown	I. Wild West
B. Omelets	F. Tennis	J. SOS
C. Humility	G. Acorns	K. Raised
D. Poring	H. Fore	L. Puff

37

HEADLINE: RACING DRIVER SIR MALCOLM CAMPBELL FIRST TO EXCEED THREE HUNDRED MILES PER HOUR.

YEAR: 1935

ANSWERS:

A. Smile	E. Soccer	I. Precedent
B. Gulliver	F. Perth	J. Serbia
C. Unmarried	G. Froth	K. Hid
D. Malcolm X	H. Red	

38

HEADLINE: NAZI POCKET BATTLESHIP GRAF SPEE LIMPS INTO MONTEVIDEO HARBOR AFTER DEFEAT BY BRITISH CRUISERS.

YEAR: 1939

ANSWERS:

A. Christie Brinkley	E. Romeo Montague	I. Flat
B. Azores	F. Dapper	J. Sprint
C. Biased	G. Tiff	K. Bate
D. Hitch	H. Bites	L. Proves

39

HEADLINE: LITTLE DAVID VICTORIOUS. HURLS STONE. KNOCKS DOWN PHILISTINE GIANT GOLIATH AND CUTS OFF HIS HEAD.

YEAR: Biblical

ANSWERS:

A. South Carolina	E. Thick	I. Chlorinated
B. Innovative	F. Dike	J. Two-fisted
C. Gunga Din	G. Host	K. Hills
D. Stupid	H. Floss	

40

HEADLINE: INVINCIBLE SPANISH ARMADA DRIVEN OUT BY BRITISH FLEET UNDER DRAKE AND HAWKINS.

YEAR: 1588

ANSWERS:

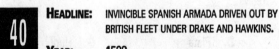

A. Academy Awards	C. Vine	E. Unbiased	G. Finnish	I. The bank
B. Rhode Island	D. Print	F. Evil	H. Rib	J. Turk

41

HEADLINE: NAPOLEON GAINS VICTORY OVER GENERAL KUTUZOV'S RUSSIANS AT BORODINO.

YEAR: 1812

ANSWERS:

A. Raging Bull	**D.** Untrue	**G.** Yoko Ono
B. Vindictive	**E.** Save	**H.** Soap
C. Sonnet	**F.** Rosa	**I.** Razors

42

HEADLINE: MCKINLEY IS ASSASSINATED BY ANARCHIST. THEODORE ROOSEVELT SUCCEEDS TO PRESIDENCY.

YEAR: 1901

ANSWERS:

A. Katharine Hepburn	**E.** Eyes	**I.** Sis
B. Iceland	**F.** Crisscross	**J.** Calamity
C. Tossed	**G.** Toe	**K.** Dove
D. Soy	**H.** Decent	

43

HEADLINE: PRESIDENT SADAT AND PRIME MINISTER BEGIN SIGN PEACE TREATY AT CAMP DAVID.

YEAR: 1979

ANSWERS:

A. Streaming	**D.** Teddy	**G.** Vested
B. Precipitate	**E.** Bet	**H.** Sam
C. Padding	**F.** An American in Paris	

44

HEADLINE: EASTERN CHRISTIAN EMPIRE FALLS AS THE TURKS CAPTURE CONSTANTINOPLE.

YEAR: 1453

ANSWERS:

A. The Scarlet Pimpernel	**D.** Stuart	**G.** Foist
B. Pancake	**E.** Hint	**H.** Sari
C. Secular	**F.** Sonnet	

45

HEADLINE: GENERAL BRADDOCK IS FATALLY WOUNDED IN FRENCH AND INDIAN AMBUSH.

YEAR: 1755

ANSWERS:

A. Buffalo Bills	**D.** Added	**G.** Awakening
B. Cheers	**E.** Drain	**H.** Mind
C. Rout	**F.** Hand	**I.** Canny

46

HEADLINE: MUTINEERS TAKE OVER BRITISH SHIP BOUNTY. CAPTAIN BLIGH AND OTHERS ARE SET ADRIFT.

YEAR: 1789

ANSWERS:

A. Don't give up the ship
B. Flintstones
C. Shiite
D. Braise
E. Harry Truman
F. Tire
G. Backboard
H. Ate

47

HEADLINE: CHIEF TECUMSEH AND CREEK INDIANS ROUTED AT HORSESHOE BEND.

YEAR: 1814

ANSWERS:

A. The horse's mouth
B. Urbane
C. Diced
D. Foe
E. The snark
F. Dice
G. Nice
H. Danes

48

HEADLINE: GYPSY ROSE LEE STRIPTEASE IS STAR ATTRACTION AT MINSKY BURLESQUE.

YEAR: 1940

ANSWERS:

A. It Ain't Necessarily So
B. Betty
C. Preempt
D. Silks
E. Quest
F. Surety
G. Roar
H. Saga

49

HEADLINE: CHIANG KAI-SHEK AND TWO MILLION SUPPORTERS FLEE MAINLAND FOR TAIWAN.

YEAR: 1949

ANSWERS:

A. We Are the World
B. Penchant
C. Knots
D. Dalai
E. King
F. Sao
G. Paul Simon
H. Infirm
I. Fail

50

HEADLINE: ENGLAND'S ROGER BANNISTER IS FIRST MAN TO BREAK FOUR MINUTES FOR MILE RUN.

YEAR: 1954

ANSWERS:

A. Aaron Burr
B. Roberts
C. Miller
D. Knitting
E. Suffer
F. Frogs
G. Danes
H. Ammunition
I. Seen

51

HEADLINE: MUHAMMAD ALI REGAINS HEAVYWEIGHT TITLE FROM JOE FRAZIER IN RETURN MATCH.

YEAR: 1974

ANSWERS:

A. Jane Fonda	E. Mirth	I. Levy
B. Maggie	F. Him	J. Crime
C. Refute	G. Lusitania	K. Her
D. Mozart	H. Wrath	

52

HEADLINE: JIMMY CONNORS WINS WIMBLEDON. POPULARIZES TWO-FISTED BACKHAND.

YEAR: 1974

ANSWERS:

A. Owl and the Pussycat	D. Swim	G. Jib
B. Zipcode	E. Moonraker	H. Mind
C. Blows	F. Finn	

53

HEADLINE: SUPERSONIC CONCORDE BEGINS FLIGHTS FROM EUROPE TO SOUTH AMERICA.

YEAR: 1976

ANSWERS:

A. Rhodesia	D. Music	G. French
B. Obfuscate	E. Moo	H. Log
C. Springsteen	F. Puerto Rico	

54

HEADLINE: CORAZON AQUINO ELECTED PHILIPPINES PRESIDENT. MARCOS GOES INTO EXILE.

YEAR: 1986

ANSWERS:

A. Indiana	E. Milton	I. Cent
B. Liquor	F. Zeppo	J. Red Sox
C. Negate	G. Chores	K. Lie
D. Spice	H. Poise	

55

HEADLINE: BUSH DEMANDS THAT IRAQ START PULLOUT FROM KUWAIT BY NOON SATURDAY.

YEAR: 1991

ANSWERS:

A. Father William	D. Husky	G. Tat
B. Torpor	E. Doubts	H. Quorum
C. Bunyan	F. Stands	I. Data

56

HEADLINE: MOST POWERFUL EARTHQUAKE IN FORTY YEARS RUMBLES THROUGH CALIFORNIA. WIDE DAMAGE IN DESERT.

YEAR: 1992

ANSWERS:
A. No place like home
B. Married
C. Dan Quayle
D. Teheran
E. Whiff
F. Bugsy
G. Fair
H. Terrorism
I. Grate
J. Studious
K. Two

57

HEADLINE: THE LORD CONFUSES LANGUAGE OF BABEL AND OF ALL EARTH. EACH NATION TO HAVE OWN LANGUAGE.

YEAR: Biblical

ANSWERS:
A. Congress of Vienna
B. Allocate
C. The Hague
D. Hale
E. Fable
F. Boa
G. Newfoundland
H Hat
I. Argonaut
J. Log

58

HEADLINE: MINUTEMEN FIGHT BRITISH AT LEXINGTON AND CONCORD. LOSSES FORCE REDCOAT RETREAT.

YEAR: 1775

ANSWERS:
A. Cardinals
B. Obstruct
C. Mexican
D. Creating
E. Totem
F. Noon
G. Fiddlers three
H. Gift-horse
I. Note

59

HEADLINE: SCIPIO AFRICANUS COUNTERATTACKS AT ZAMA. CARTHAGINIANS SURRENDER.

YEAR: 202 BC

ANSWERS:
A. Diane Keaton
B. Ramification
C. Zag
D. Caspian Sea
E. Runts
F. Crust
G. Arras
H. Crutch

60

HEADLINE: CHARLOTTETOWN CONFERENCE DISCUSSES FORMATION OF DOMINION OF CANADA.

YEAR: 1864

ANSWERS:
A. Cocoon
B. From Russia
C. Sacco
D. Facile
E. News
F. Fomented
G. North
H. Ado
I. Intoned
J. Faint

61

HEADLINE: ROEBLING AND SON COMPLETE NEW SUSPENSION-TYPE BROOKLYN BRIDGE.

YEAR: 1883

ANSWERS:
A. Colorado Springs
B. Benign
C. Penny
D. Boulder
E. Sky
F. Milton
G. Pew
H. Stone
I. Bee

62

HEADLINE: RED ARMY COMMANDER IN CHIEF CHU TEH DEFEATS CHIANG'S NATIONALISTS.

YEAR: 1949

ANSWERS:
A. Timothy Dalton
B. Chaucer
C. Agassi
D. March
E. Diner
F. Manifest
G. Fend
H. Chinese

63

HEADLINE: FIRST USE OF CAT SCANNER PROMISES TO REVOLUTIONIZE X-RAY DIAGNOSIS.

YEAR: 1973

ANSWERS:
A. Venezuela
B. Faction
C. Rosetta stone
D. Soirs
E. Miss
F. Cord
G. Xiaoping
H. Sir
I. Fury

64

HEADLINE: SCUD ATTACKS ON TWO SAUDI CITIES ARE FOILED BY PATRIOT MISSILES.

YEAR: 1991

ANSWERS:
A. Moby Dick
B. Illustrious
C. Fiesta
D. Static
E. Wondered
F. Aspic
G. Oat
H. Siesta

65

HEADLINE: JONAH FALLS OVERBOARD IN STORM AND IS SWALLOWED BY GREAT WHALE.

YEAR: Biblical

ANSWERS:
A. Whitney
B. Belabor
C. Flood
D. Moons
E. Jail
F. Wrangler
G. Dash
H. Sat
I. Waves
J. Lard

66

HEADLINE: COLONIALS BOARD BRITISH SHIPS AND DUMP TEA CARGO INTO BOSTON HARBOR.

YEAR: 1773

ANSWERS:

A. Not to praise him
B. Bono
C. Oslo
D. Dracula
E. Bardot
F. Cribs
G. Poignant
H. Brash
I. Dish

67

HEADLINE: STONEWALL JACKSON DIES IN INDECISIVE BATTLE AT CHANCELLORSVILLE.

YEAR: 1863

ANSWERS:

A. Class action
B. Javelin
C. Volatile
D. Wreck
E. Tint
F. Disobedience
G. Halls
H. Lens

68

HEADLINE: TWENTY-SECOND AMENDMENT IS RATIFIED. NO PERSON SHALL BE ELECTED PRESIDENT MORE THAN TWICE.

YEAR: 1951

ANSWERS:

A. And that's the way it is
B. Peters
C. Eminent
D. Cooper
E. Last Minstrel
F. Decide
G. Fend
H. Conmen
I. Need
J. Bowler

69

HEADLINE: FRENCH GRANT INDEPENDENCE TO ALGERIA. BEN BELLA IS FIRST PRESIDENT.

YEAR: 1962

ANSWERS:

A. Paris
B. Darling
C. Ghent
D. Proliferate
E. Candle
F. Fences
G. Inner
H. Ebb tide
I. Sent

70

HEADLINE: HUNDREDS OF PRIVATE VESSELS CARRY CUBAN REFUGEES TO KEY WEST.

YEAR: 1980

ANSWERS:

A. Final four
B. Weather
C. Puck
D. Seventy
E. Dress
F. Surrogates
G. Bevy
H. Cedes

71

HEADLINE: WEATHER FORECASTERS ANTICIPATE FORTY DAYS AND FORTY NIGHTS OF RAIN WITHOUT LETUP.

YEAR: Biblical

ANSWERS:

A. Poison
B. Consecrate
C. Trusty
D. Daniel Defoe
E. Thaw
F. Parity
G. Tasting
H. Wharf
I. Harte
J. Iffy
K. Trout

72

HEADLINE: SERPENT FOUND GUILTY. SENTENCED TO CRAWL UPON BELLY AND EAT DUST FOR LIFE.

YEAR: Biblical

ANSWERS:

A. Warren Beatty
B. Stones
C. Neptune
D. Pristine
E. Cloud
F. Dot
G. Gulf of Aden
H. Culled
I. Fly

73

HEADLINE: KING CAROL OF ROMANIA ABDICATES AND GOES INTO EXILE.

YEAR: 1940

ANSWERS:

A. Franks
B. Maine
C. Exciting
D. Abate
E. Laos
F. Radio
G. Cooling
H. Ode

74

HEADLINE: PRESIDENT LINCOLN IS SHOT AND KILLED AT FORD'S THEATRE. ASSASSIN ESCAPES.

YEAR: 1865

ANSWERS:

A. Reconcile
B. Nathan Hale
C. Kissed
D. Tresses
E. Lassie
F. Pass
G. Lands
H. Fit to print
I. Odd

75

HEADLINE: JACK NICKLAUS WINS THE MASTERS GOLF CHAMPIONSHIP AT AUGUSTA, GEORGIA.

YEAR: 1965

ANSWERS:

A. Thomas
B. Negligence
C. Task
D. Its stomach
E. Pours
F. Huck
G. Jai alai
H. Fur
I. Paging
J. Saw

76

HEADLINE: ISRAELIS DRIVE SYRIANS BACK TO WITHIN EIGHTEEN MILES OF DAMASCUS.

YEAR: 1973

ANSWERS:

A. Ankara
B. Sirius
C. Modem

D. Vacillates
E. Wishing
F. Niece

G. Bides
H. Thirsty
I. Foes

77

HEADLINE: MARAT IS STABBED TO DEATH IN HIS BATH BY CHARLOTTE CORDAY.

YEAR: 1793

ANSWERS:

A. Colombia
B. Attrition
C. Chary

D. Darth
E. Bathed
F. Hasty

G. Abets
H. Beds

78

HEADLINE: HAITI PRESIDENT HENRI CHRISTOPHE FACES REVOLT AND COMMITS SUICIDE.

YEAR: 1820

ANSWERS:

A. Irish
B. Counterfeit
C. Vicar

D. Dish
E. Chides
F. Compass

G. Dim
H. The antelope
I. Inert

79

HEADLINE: DAVY CROCKETT AND JIM BOWIE AMONG TEXANS WIPED OUT BY MEXICANS AT ALAMO.

YEAR: 1836

ANSWERS:

A. Red Wings
B. Woman I love
C. Taxicab
D. Except

E. Dummy
F. Moan
G. Ado

H. Jettison
I. Baa
J. Tacky

80

HEADLINE: CUSTER AND ENTIRE FORCE WIPED OUT BY SIOUX UNDER CRAZY HORSE AT LITTLE BIG HORN.

YEAR: 1876

ANSWERS:

A. Alexandria
B. Torrid zone
C. Wither
D. Court

E. Duty
F. Buying
G. Tet

H. Reprehensible
I. Fuss
J. Coco

81

HEADLINE: CORBETT KNOCKS OUT SULLIVAN TO BECOME FIRST HEAVYWEIGHT KING UNDER NEW QUEENSBERRY RULES.

YEAR: 1892

ANSWERS:

A. Venetian	**E.** Unsound	**I.** Buckeye
B. Quibble	**F.** Egg	**J.** Forty
C. Whistler's mother	**G.** Snicker-snack	**K.** Wet
D. Louvre	**H.** Rot	

82

HEADLINE: CHEVROLET-DESIGNED RACING CAR WINS INDIANAPOLIS FIVE HUNDRED.

YEAR: 1920

ANSWERS:

A. Edward VIII	**D.** Roving	**G.** Dancing
B. Unicef	**E.** Clandestine	**H.** Old
C. Sphere	**F.** Rash	

83

HEADLINE: COMMANDER RICHARD BYRD AND PILOT FLOYD BENNETT FLY TO NORTH POLE. CIRCLE TOP OF WORLD.

YEAR: 1926

ANSWERS:

A. Cape Horn	**E.** Dint	**I.** Martyr
B. Cynical	**F.** Told	**J.** Bold
C. Pimpernel	**G.** Cotton	**K.** Followed
D. Brother	**H.** Dry	**L.** Doff

84

HEADLINE: MUSSOLINI SON-IN-LAW COUNT GALEAZZO CIANO IS NAMED ITALY'S FOREIGN MINISTER.

YEAR: 1936

ANSWERS:

A. Clementine	**C.** Swizzle	**E.** Staying	**G.** Russian	**I.** Coat
B. Fusion	**D.** Nominal	**F.** Asia	**H.** Drooling	**J.** Moi

85

HEADLINE: TOBRUK FALLS TO ROMMEL. SERIOUS LOSS TO ALLIES. BRITISH DIG IN AS NAZIS NEAR EGYPTIAN BORDER.

YEAR: 1942

ANSWERS:

A. Painstaking	**E.** Three little maids	**I.** Sirs
B. Zagreb	**F.** Oro	**J.** Business
C. Solo	**G.** Fundy	**K.** Oral
D. Baltimore	**H.** Roils	

86

HEADLINE: POPE JOHN XXIII DIES IN VATICAN. HIS REIGN CHAMPIONED PEACE AND CHRISTIAN UNITY.

YEAR: 1963

ANSWERS:

A. Sixpence	E. Unchain	H. Hit
B. Periphery	F. Poi	I. Death and taxes
C. Indiana	G. Jingoism	J. Coin
D. Vici		

87

HEADLINE: FIVE-TIME BATTING CHAMPION ROBERTO CLEMENTE IS KILLED IN AIR CRASH.

YEAR: 1972

ANSWERS:

A. Let them eat cake	D. Imperial	G. Sin
B. Romeo	E. Strife	H. Catch
C. Irving	F. Blini	I. Bond

88

HEADLINE: FORD GIVES PARDON TO NIXON. FORMER PRESIDENT EXPRESSES REGRETS FOR MISTAKES.

YEAR: 1974

ANSWERS:

A. Redskins	E. Spoof	H. Pete Sampras
B. Goering	F. Friend	I. Son
C. Extrovert	G. Mess	J. Terror
D. Fixed		

89

HEADLINE: RICHARD NIXON LEAVES WHITE HOUSE. BIDS EMOTIONAL FAREWELL TO WASHINGTON.

YEAR: 1974

ANSWERS:

A. Botswana	E. Towers	I. Ruth
B. Longfellow	F. Hone	J. Idi Amin
C. Servile	G. Sadat	K. Echo
D. Nix	H. Hie	

90

HEADLINE: TURKEY LANDS ARMED FORCE IN CYPRUS. DROPS PARATROOPERS INTO NICOSIA AREA.

YEAR: 1974

ANSWERS:

A. Nittany Lions	D. Parody	G. Dick Francis
B. Mercedes	E. Spout	H. Apropos
C. Aurora	F. Rare	

91

HEADLINE: FEDERAL GRAND JURY INDICTS SEVEN NIXON
AIDES ON WATERGATE CONSPIRACY CHARGES.

YEAR: 1974

ANSWERS:
A. Andrew Johnson
B. Confidence
C. Exacting
D. Gritty
E. Slurred
F. Prissy
G. Diva
H. Aegean Sea
I. Car

92

HEADLINE: GIANT STATUE OF SUN GOD COLOSSUS OF
RHODES COLLAPSES IN EARTHQUAKE.

YEAR: 224 BC

ANSWERS:
A. Graceland
B. Liechtenstein
C. Hook
D. Sass
E. Outdo
F. Fats
G. Querulous
H. Spoof
I. Gas

93

HEADLINE: PROMETHEUS BOUND OPENS. NEW AESCHYLUS
DRAMA IS SMASH HIT.

YEAR: 460 BC

ANSWERS:
A. Bert Lahr
B. Specious
C. Pious
D. Shaws
E. Study
F. Anne
G. Mohammed
H. Hens

94

HEADLINE: EMPEROR CLAUDIUS IS DEAD. WAS POISONED BY
WIFE AGRIPPINA.

YEAR: 54 AD

ANSWERS:
A. Radio Days
B. Digress
C. Public
D. New-mown
E. Aida
F. Pupae
G. Fire
H. Poise

95

HEADLINE: BLACKBEARD THE PIRATE IS KILLED AS HIS
SHIP IS TAKEN BY BRITISH FORCE.

YEAR: 1718

ANSWERS:
A. Frills
B. Risk
C. At the Races
D. Splash
E. Hark
F. Beside
G. Baby
H. Die
I. Hopi
J. Kinetic
K. Bit

96 **HEADLINE:** LINDY DOES IT. CHARLES LINDBERGH FLIES ATLANTIC NONSTOP TO PARIS THROUGH SNOW AND SLEET.

YEAR: 1927

ANSWERS:

A. Pablo Picasso	E. Hints	H. Tolls
B. Transient	F. Dirt	I. Unfasten
C. Howls	G. Horace Greeley	J. Hind
D. Toddling		

97 **HEADLINE:** BRITISH SOLDIERS FIRE ON HARASSING MOB. ELEVEN CASUALTIES IN BOSTON MASSACRE.

YEAR: 1770

ANSWERS:

A. Marlon Brando	D. Hisses	G. Lee
B. Fairies	E. Sevens	H. Scores
C. Stagnation	F. British Columbia	

98 **HEADLINE:** JEFFERSON DAVIS IS NAMED CONFEDERACY PRESIDENT. MONTGOMERY IS CAPITAL.

YEAR: 1861

ANSWERS:

A. Montpelier	D. Prince of Tides	G. Jane Grey
B. Ascendancy	E. Miss	H. Dove
C. Amor	F. Distaff	

99 **HEADLINE:** MARXIST SALVADOR ALLENDE IS ELECTED TO THE PRESIDENCY OF CHILE.

YEAR: 1970

ANSWERS:

A. Adam and Eve	D. Erie	G. Shell
B. Sixty	E. Lesotho	H. Freer
C. Didactic	F. Polls	I. Cent

 100 **HEADLINE:** RADIOACTIVE FALLOUT FROM CHERNOBYL DISASTER IS SCATTERED OVER WIDE AREA.

YEAR: 1986

ANSWERS:

A. Mailer	E. Roses	H. Stated
B. Silverado	F. Bawled	I. Cute
C. Caviar	G. Rodeo	J. Rhetoric
D. Tiffany		

MORE SMART WORD PRODUCTS AVAILABLE FROM

THE PRINCETON REVIEW

The Princeton Review and Random House, Inc., present a full range of products that can help anyone build an educated vocabulary and improve diction. From audio cassettes to crossword puzzles, The Princeton Review is your best bet for improving your command of the language.

Usage Guide from Villard Books:

WORD SMART I and II
by Adam Robinson and the
staff of Princeton Review

ISBN: 0-679-74589-0, volume I
ISBN: 0-679-73863-0, volume II
$10.00 each, paperback

GRAMMAR SMART
by the staff of
The Princeton Review

ISBN: 0-679-74617-X
$9.00 paperback

Audio Cassettes from Living Language:

WORD SMART CASSETTES
by Adam Robinson and
Julian Fleischer

ISBN: 0-517-59355-6
$25.00 4 60-minute cassettes

GRAMMAR SMART CASSETTES
by Julian Fleischer and the
staff of The Princeton Review

ISBN: 0-517-59545-1
$25.00 4 60-minute cassettes

Ask your local bookseller or call 1-800-733-3000